Join AAA Today and Let Our Travel Professionals Take The Complications Out of Vacations!

Y0-CXP-991

We can help you with:

- Complete travel agency services, including expert travel planning and all travel reservations
- Passport Photos and International Driving Permits
- Fee-Free American Express® Travelers Cheques
- Discounts on Avis and Hertz Car Rentals
- Hotel Reservations
- Rail Tickets
- Individual and Escorted Tours

- Travel Insurance
- Tour Operator Default Protection Plan
- TripAssist, including 24-hour emergency access to legal, medical and travel related services worldwide
- AND Emergency Road Service Abroad — AAA maintains reciprocal agreements with auto clubs in 20 countries on five continents around the world

To Join AAA Today Just Call 1-800-336-4357

☐ **YES!** I want to learn how a Triple-A membership can take the complications out of vacations. Please send me FREE information at no obligation.

NAME _____

ADDRESS _____

_____

CITY _____ STATE _____ ZIP _____

PHONE _____

(Membership is available only to residents of the USA and Canada)

GPA 96

Discover the Benefits of Membership BEFORE You Take Your Next Trip.

Complete the postage-paid reply card TODAY.

AA

GLOVEBOX ATLAS

GERMANY

AUSTRIA & SWITZERLAND

contents

Map pages	ii
Map symbols	iii
Route planner	iv
Distance chart	I
Road atlas	2-39
Index and city environs plans	40-60

Berlin	41	Salzburg	55
Bern	42	Wien	59
Köln	49	Zürich	60
München	51		

1st edition February 1996

© The Automobile Association 1996

Published by AA Publishing (a trading name of Automobile Association Developments Limited, whose registered office is Norfolk House, Priestley Road, Basingstoke, Hampshire, RG24 9NY. Registered number 1878835).

Mapping produced by the Cartographic Department of The Automobile Association. This atlas has been compiled and produced from the Automaps database utilising electronic and computer technology.

ISBN 0 7495 1187 7

A CIP catalogue for this book is available from the British Library.

Printed in Great Britain by BPC Waterlow Ltd, Dunstable.

The contents of this atlas are believed correct at the time of printing. Nevertheless, the publishers cannot accept any responsibility for errors or omissions or for changes in the details given. They would welcome information to help keep this atlas up to date, please write to the Cartographic Editor, Publishing Division, The Automobile Association, Norfolk House, Priestley Road, Basingstoke, Hampshire, RG24 9NY.

map pages

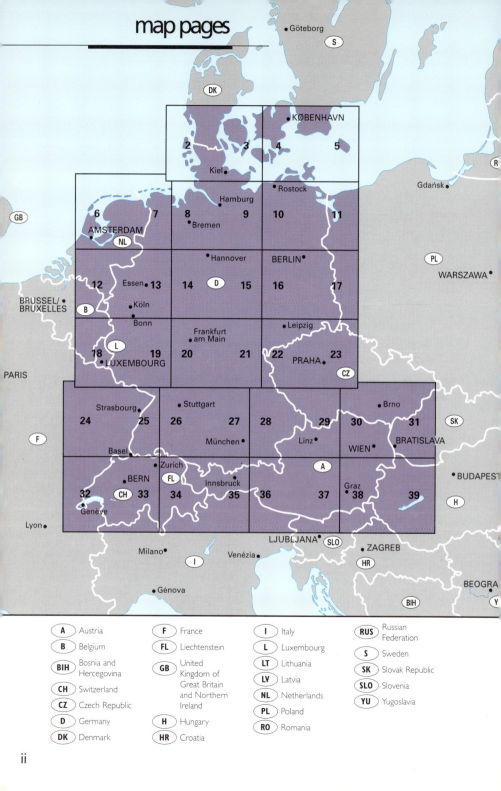

A	Austria	F	France
B	Belgium	FL	Liechtenstein
BIH	Bosnia and Hercegovina	GB	United Kingdom of Great Britain and Northern Ireland
CH	Switzerland		
CZ	Czech Republic	H	Hungary
D	Germany	HR	Croatia
DK	Denmark		

I	Italy
L	Luxembourg
LT	Lithuania
LV	Latvia
NL	Netherlands
PL	Poland
RO	Romania

RUS	Russian Federation
S	Sweden
SK	Slovak Republic
SLO	Slovenia
YU	Yugoslavia

map symbols

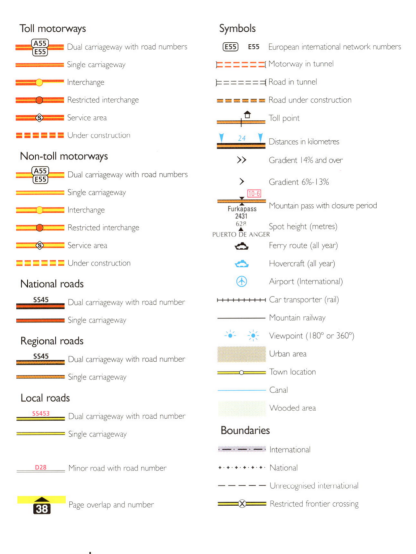

Toll motorways

- A55 / E55 — Dual carriageway with road numbers
- Single carriageway
- Interchange
- Restricted interchange
- (S) Service area
- Under construction

Non-toll motorways

- A55 / E55 — Dual carriageway with road numbers
- Single carriageway
- Interchange
- Restricted interchange
- (S) Service area
- Under construction

National roads

- SS45 — Dual carriageway with road number
- Single carriageway

Regional roads

- SS45 — Dual carriageway with road number
- Single carriageway

Local roads

- SS453 — Dual carriageway with road number
- Single carriageway
- D28 — Minor road with road number

- 38 — Page overlap and number

Symbols

- E55 E55 European international network numbers
- Motorway in tunnel
- Road in tunnel
- Road under construction
- Toll point
- 24 Distances in kilometres
- >> Gradient 14% and over
- > Gradient 6%-13%
- 10-6 Furkapass 2431 Mountain pass with closure period
- 628 PUERTO DE ANGER Spot height (metres)
- Ferry route (all year)
- Hovercraft (all year)
- Airport (International)
- +++++++ Car transporter (rail)
- Mountain railway
- Viewpoint (180° or 360°)
- Urban area
- Town location
- Canal
- Wooded area

Boundaries

- International
- National
- Unrecognised international
- Restricted frontier crossing

scale

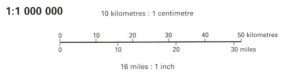

route planner

distance chart

Chemnitz - Rostock = 499 km

499

Cities (in order along the diagonal):

Amsterdam (NL), Basel (CH), Berlin (D), Bern (CH), Bonn (D), Bratislava (SK), Bremen (D), Brno (CZ), Brussel/Bruxelles (B), Chemnitz (D), Dresden (D), Erfurt (D), Essen (D), Frankfurt am Main (D), Genève (CH), Graz (A), Hamburg (D), Hannover (D), Innsbruck (A), Kiel (D), Klagenfurt (A), Köln (D), Leipzig (D), Linz (A), Ljubljana (SLO), Lübeck (D), Luxembourg (L), Lyon (F), Milano (I), München (D), Nürnberg (D), Praha (CZ), Regensburg (D), Rostock (D), Salzburg (A), Strasbourg (F), Stuttgart (D), Wien (A), Zagreb (HR), Zürich (CH)

To \ From	Amsterdam (NL)	Basel (CH)	Berlin (D)	Bern (CH)	Bonn (D)	Bratislava (SK)	Bremen (D)	Brno (CZ)	Brussel/Bruxelles (B)	Chemnitz (D)	Dresden (D)	Erfurt (D)	Essen (D)	Frankfurt am Main (D)	Genève (CH)	Graz (A)	Hamburg (D)	Hannover (D)	Innsbruck (A)	Kiel (D)	Klagenfurt (A)	Köln (D)	Leipzig (D)	Linz (A)	Ljubljana (SLO)	Lübeck (D)	Luxembourg (L)	Lyon (F)	Milano (I)	München (D)	Nürnberg (D)	Praha (CZ)	Regensburg (D)	Rostock (D)	Salzburg (A)	Strasbourg (F)	Stuttgart (D)	Wien (A)	Zagreb (HR)
Basel (CH)	653																																						
Berlin (D)	841	864																																					
Bern (CH)	289	92	957																																				
Bonn (D)	1232	478	596	570																																			
Bratislava (SK)	354	915	675	932	961																																		
Bremen (D)	1172	764	388	856	340	1151																																	
Brno (CZ)	210	581	773	674	984	130	833																																
Brussel/Bruxelles (B)	730	672	260	765	554	1187	497	1127																															
Chemnitz (D)	444	554	500	554	493	231	231	584	716																														
Dresden (D)	1004	740	194	832	430	1037	333	978	357	784																													
Erfurt (D)	1162	330	525	260	568	94	251	231	463	579																													
Essen (D)	466	578	308	525	544	1119	164	733	194	722	1117																												
Frankfurt am Main (D)	375	817	289	909	452	1181	121	881	322	594	1081	256																											
Genève (CH)	1001	671	281	763	317	1035	123	726	494	523	1019	208	958																										
Graz (A)	552	389	750	406	730	550	550	602	956	920	443	378	1105	443																									
Hamburg (D)	1186	914	387	1006	538	1278	27	1141	210	313	210	915	378	1141	210																								
Hannover (D)	262	754	494	935	771	1238	178	508	987	467	313	977	27	467	313	708																							
Innsbruck (A)	639	494	569	587	949	310	901	190	212	374	977	310	591	949	310	591	127																						
Kiel (D)	994	184	800	27	591	774	1012	732	734	467	512	952	331	493	774	151	110	151																					
Klagenfurt (A)	1247	387	743	492	258	913	774	711	1030	1307	208	331	943	312	797	556	585	585	622																				
Köln (D)	523	996	694	723	439	1166	287	1248	981	734	840	409	739	354	221	943	799	838	875	808																			
Leipzig (D)	413	874	996	330	976	439	1287	916	1097	494	426	274	493	267	404	1196	810	1053	838	875	838																		
Leipzig/Linz... (Linz A)	935	707	764	966	461	1238	190	508	811	580	426	271	333	404	267	510	231	663	472	425	640	677																	

Ljubljana (SLO)	1082	1237	184	1006	711	1248	1030	1307	981	1097	494	705	876	722	1004	398	637	389	151	887	322	663	911	951															
Lübeck (D)	834	1033	387	583	424	563	916	811	1097	916	705	580	348	580	163	783	640	425	462	397	586	389	785	912	887														
Luxembourg (L)	664	583	431	431	531	424	563	563	509	753	789	271	409	333	467	226	508	409	271	274	333	274	226	310	212	619													
Lyon (F)	438	431	531	531	393	521	509	753	753	512	366	518	333	518	332	693	530	469	542	675	542	243	310	310	243	619	619												
Milano (I)	967	821	346	821	329	628	696	205	682	628	472	243	243	262	549	984	773	379	152	922	225	672	696	747	1102	941	382	307											
München (D)	763	617	492	617	393	492	682	464	1030	718	508	233	355	243	290	779	568	354	354	391	508	769	542	897	683	123	259	102											
Nürnberg (D)	645	492	232	492	1088	300	804	494	1238	300	380	183	233	355	475	401	962	325	568	354	391	779	640	1173	897	336	117	799	456	579									
Praha (CZ)	977	431	726	571	372	896	682	300	538	932	134	569	723	569	180	926	780	258	725	540	783	278	723	983	1102	878	573	309	186	556	811	610							
Regensburg (D)	632	346	492	492	696	205	653	629	823	431	882	763	355	471	560	706	401	768	219	494	727	327	644	788	763	219	102	259	377	266	307	382	941	
Rostock (D)	621	492	617	617	492	464	602	718	1097	641	183	1203	329	524	670	626	1106	195	202	426	350	508	472	639	497	206	292	376	825	518	413	885	825	518	922	
Salzburg (A)	1157	1092	617	1072	63	886	657	127	1262	423	902	317	902	749	183	941	960	719	717	446	748	962	434	496	294	396	336	1173	856	434	496	294	396	856	1102	297	
Strasbourg (F)	1343	844	1072	969	429	866	815	1298	494	1262	904	223	935	402	135	1349	1133	629	335	1058	223	1089	402	135	1349	1133	629	549	719	662	582	418	1288	1058	629	549	719	662	928
Zürich (CH)	854	105	844	122	583	815	866	869	686	656	723	684	660	435	285	776	922	284	474	577	600	687	979	771	438	306	286	445	1040	252	219	740	904						

5

Höör
E22
Tollarp
28
118
E22
32
Åhus
Kristianstad
30
23
13
11
Hörby
6/19
Yngsjö
17
Eslöv
12
Hörby
Hanöbukten
E22
Hurva
10
27
Maglehem
Harlösa
104
13
Kristinehov
Brösarp
Vitemölla
Dalby
24
11
Sjöbo
24
St
Olof
28
Veberöd
102
Tranås
19
9
Vik
Sturup
16
13
Simrishamn
59
E65
Sövestad
19
Tomelilla
29
11
Garsnas
nderslov
Skurup
9
Borrby
Skillinge
101
Ystad
Löderup
47
Abbekås
Beddingestrand
Sandhammaren
Smygehamn

Hammerodde
Sandvig
Allinge
150
Gudhjem
Hasle
24
14
158
Klemensker
Svaneke
Østerlars
Østermarie
Rønne
38
Åkirkeby
9
Neksø
30
Bornholm
Snogebæk
Dueodde

Kap Arkona
enkirchen

Glowe
Sagard
Sassnitz
251
Neu Mukran
196
Rügen
Binz
Sellin
Putbus
Göhren
Thiessow
Greifswalder
Bodden
Peenemünde

1 : 1 000 000

0   10   20   30   40   50 km

11

D   E   F
Kołobrzeg

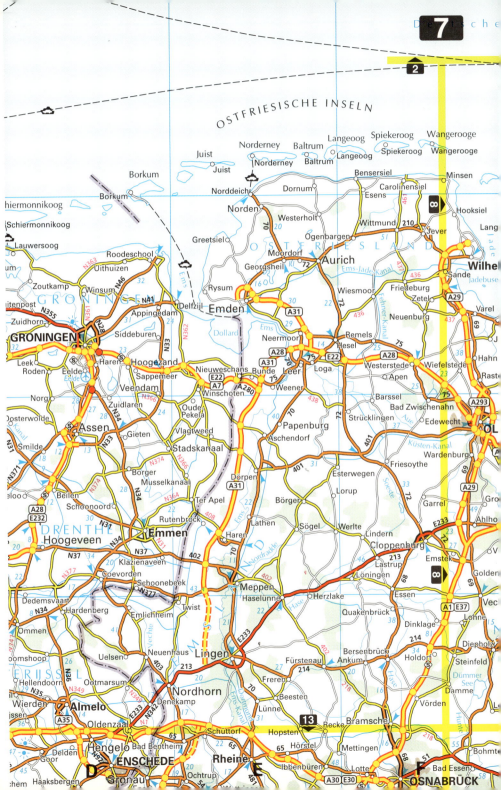

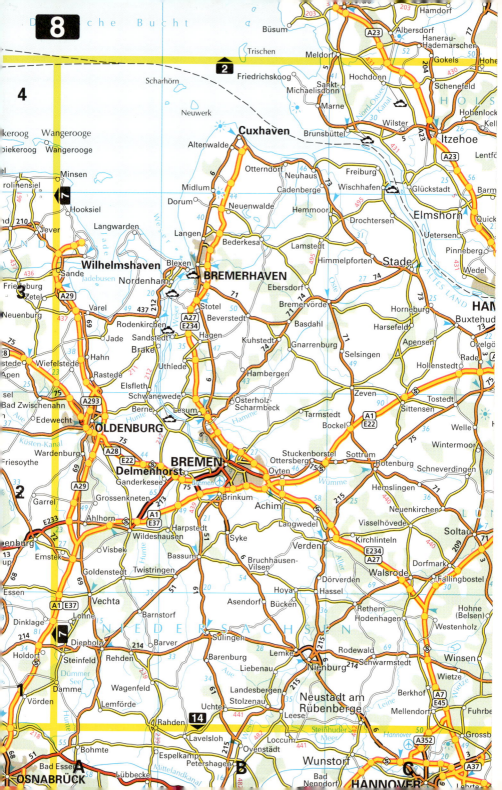

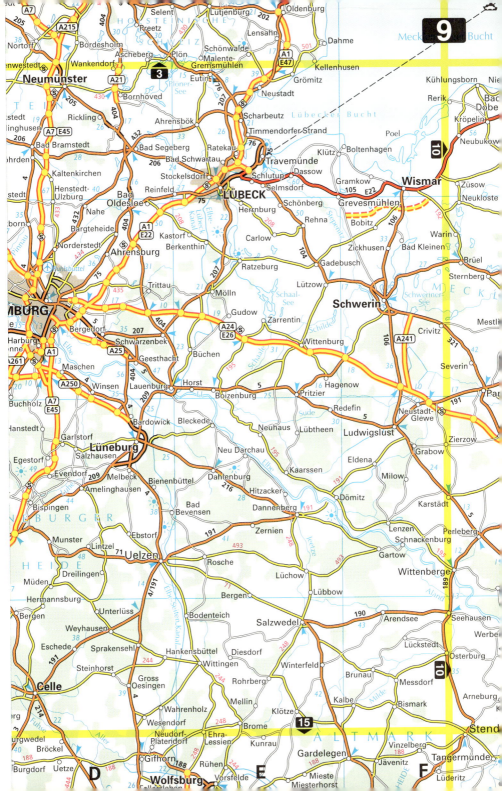

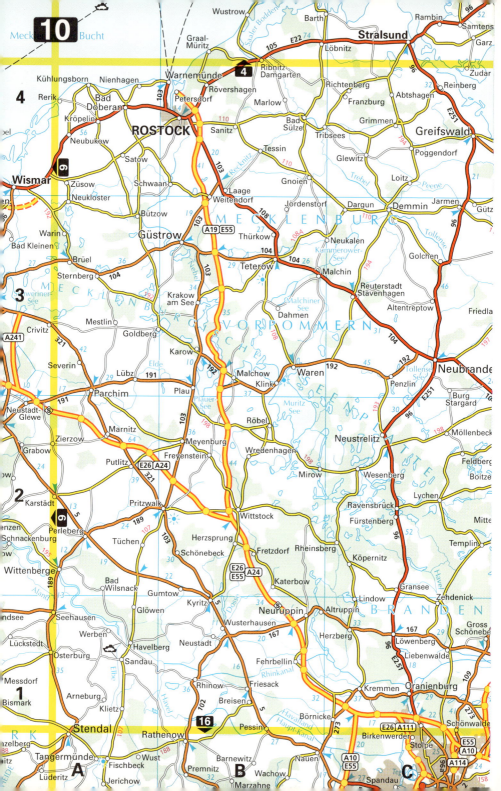

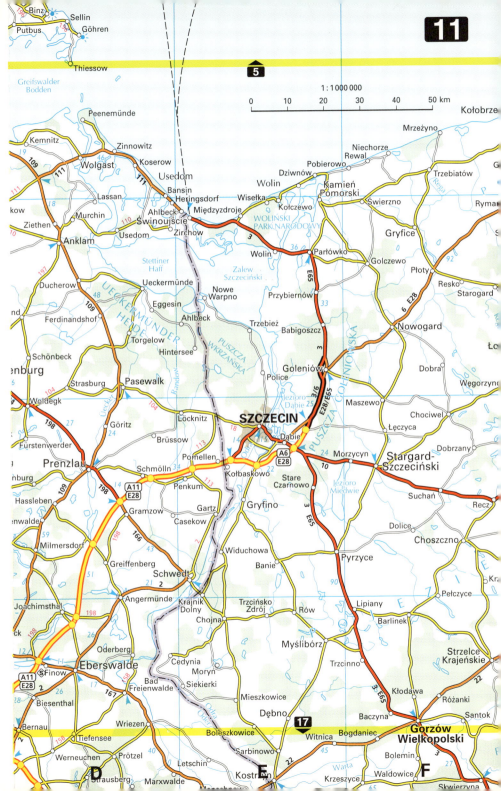

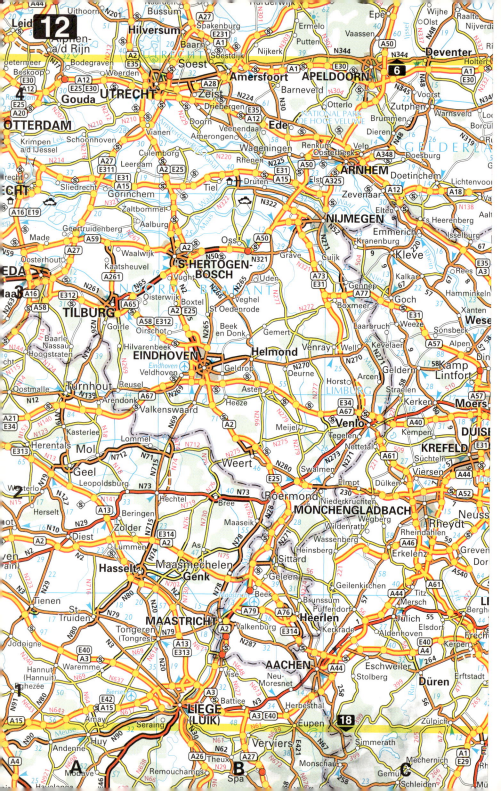

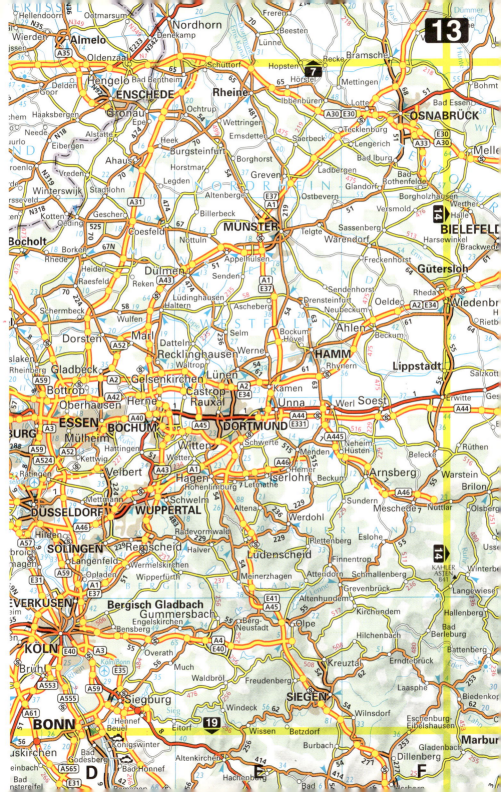

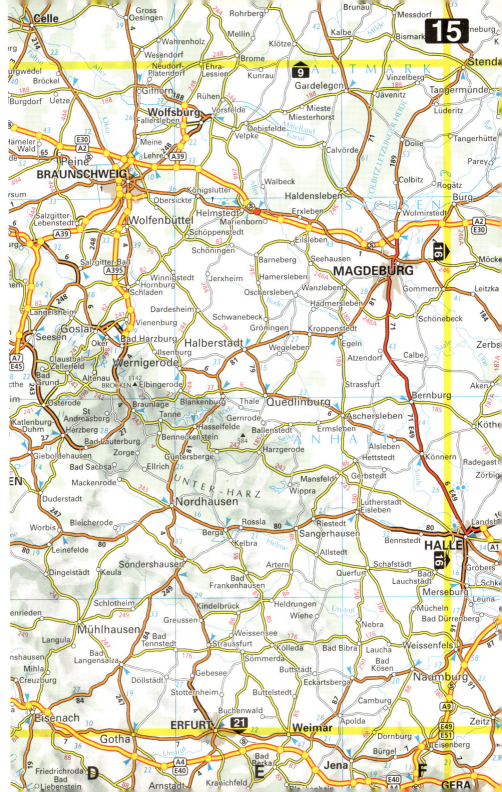

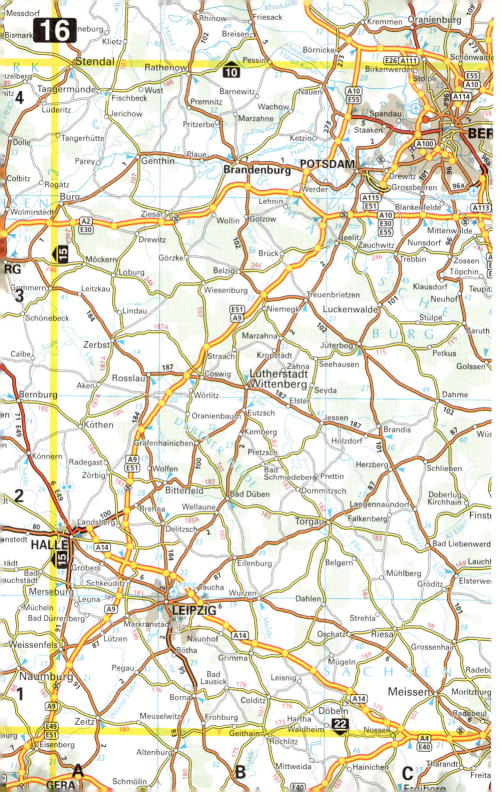

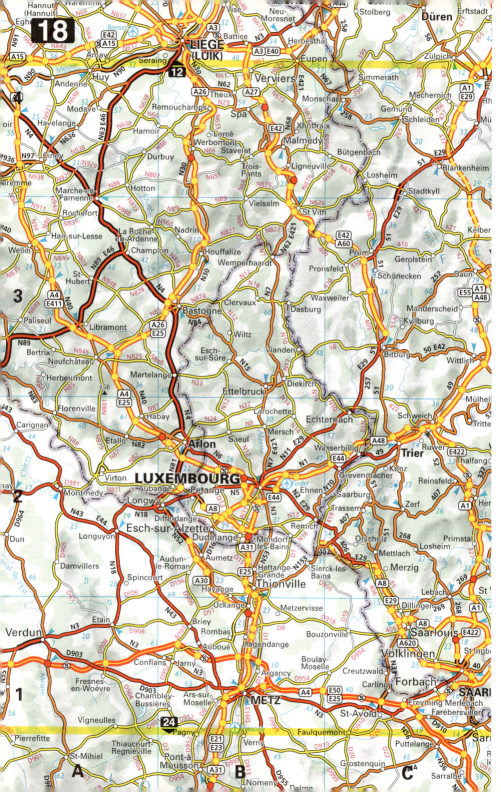

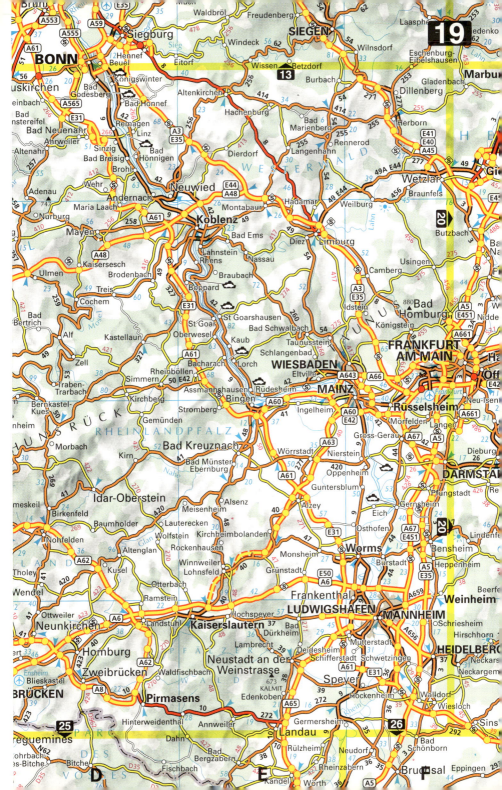

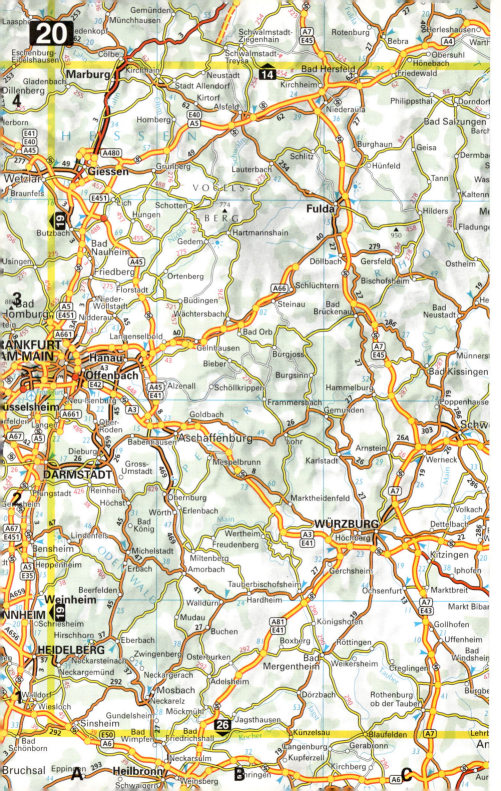

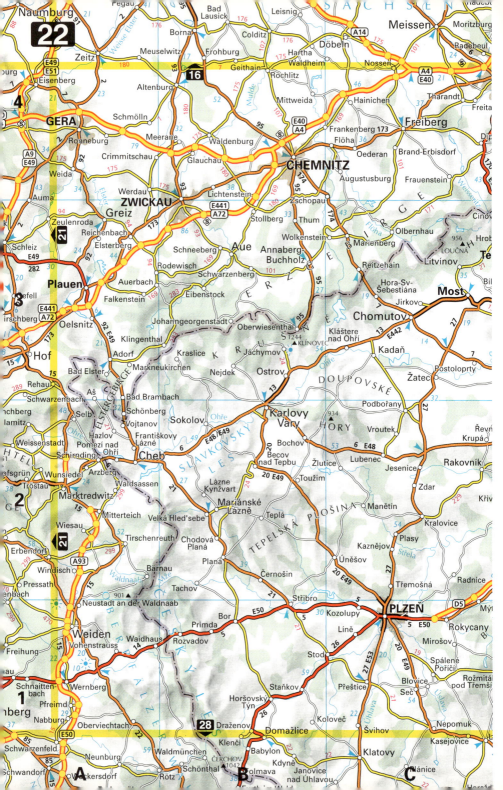

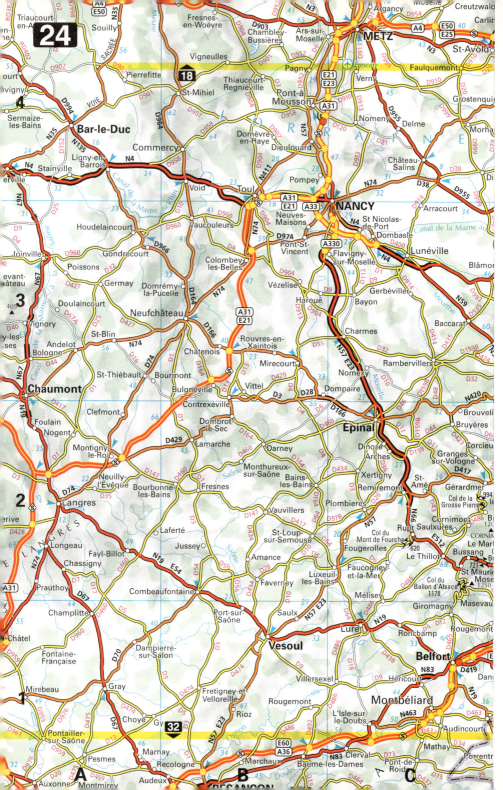

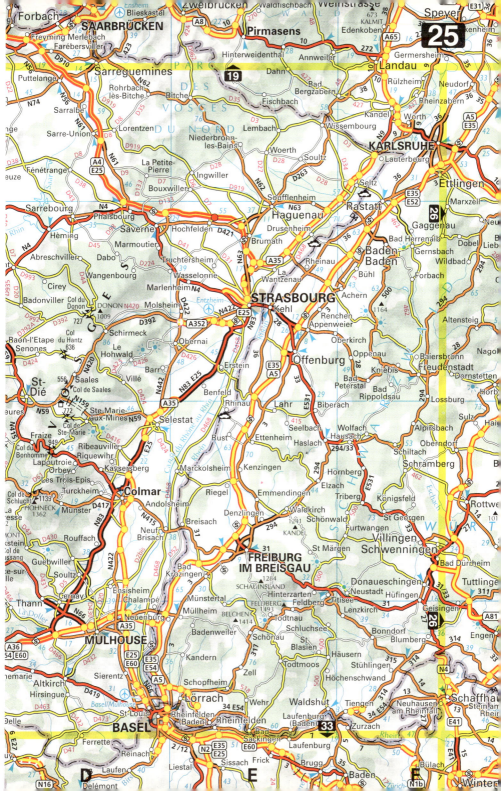

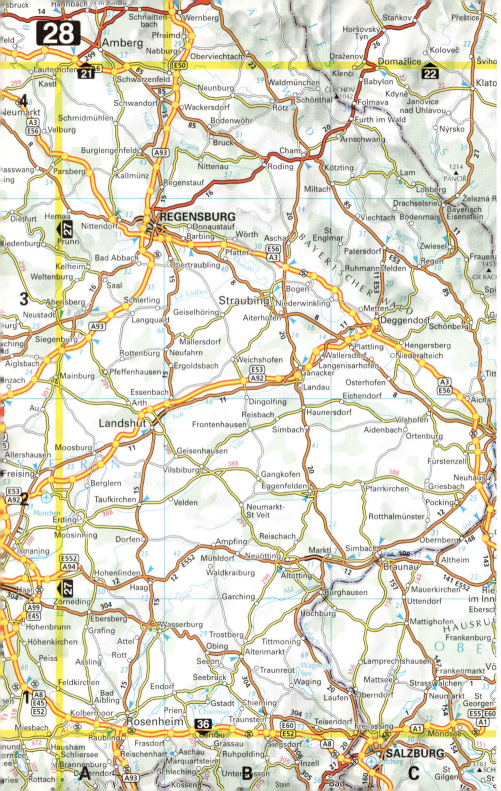

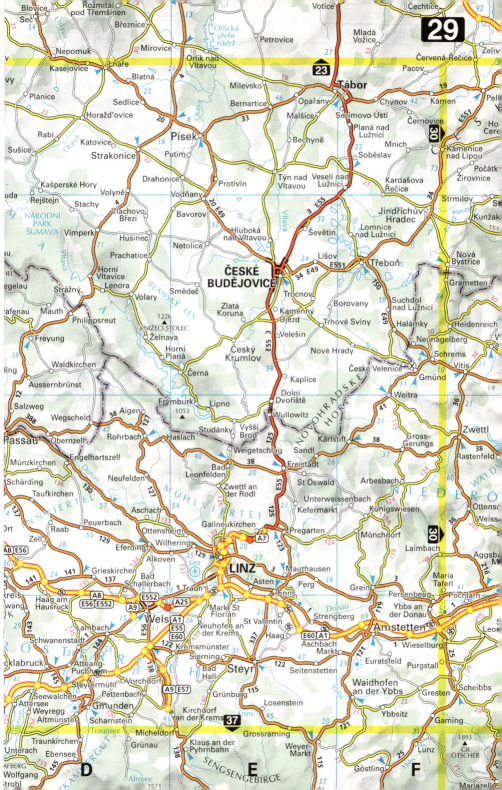

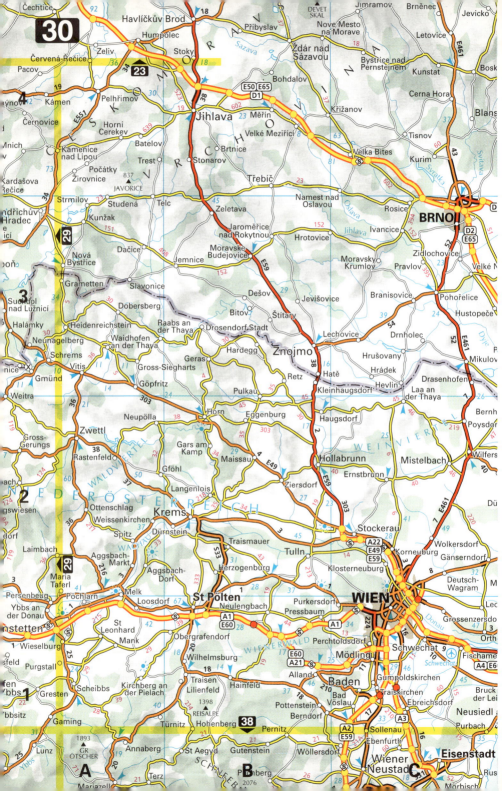

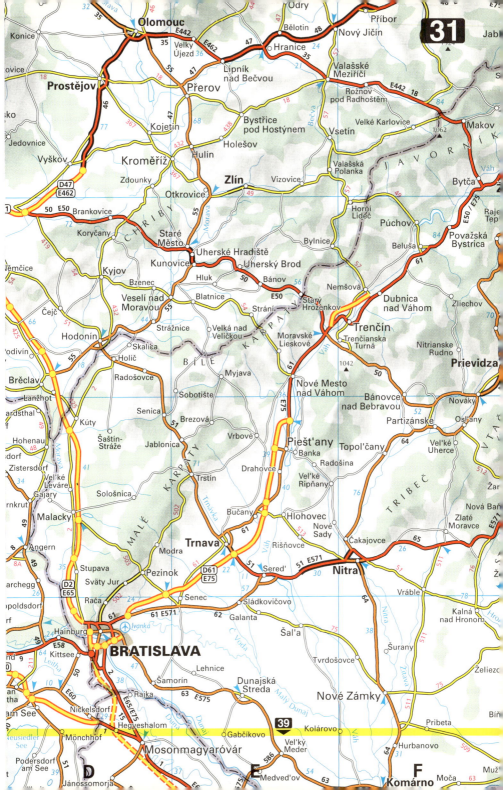

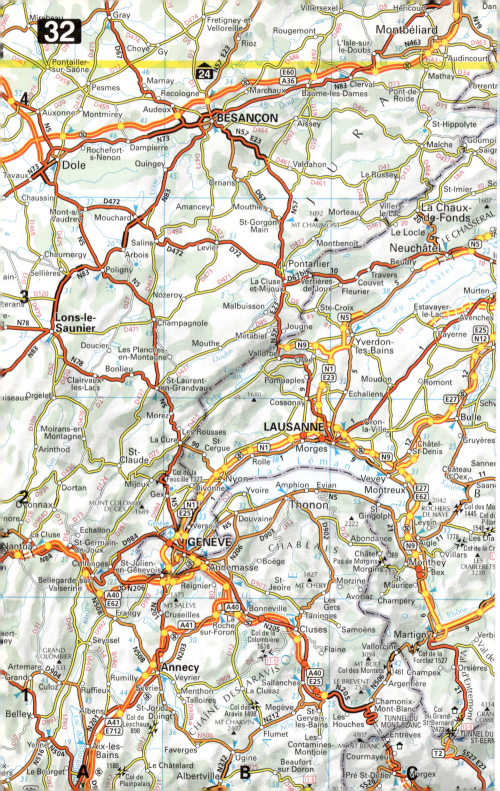

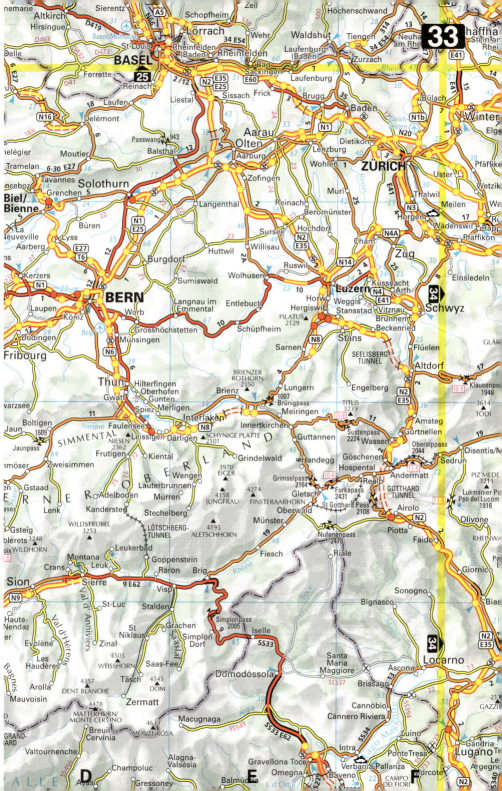

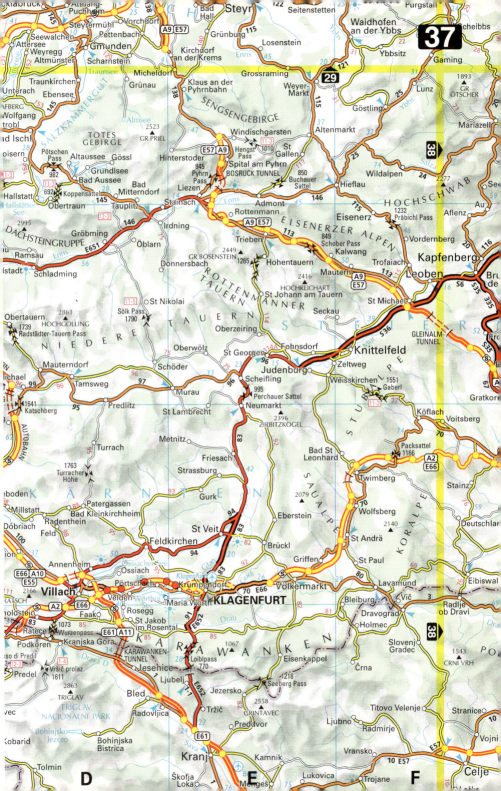

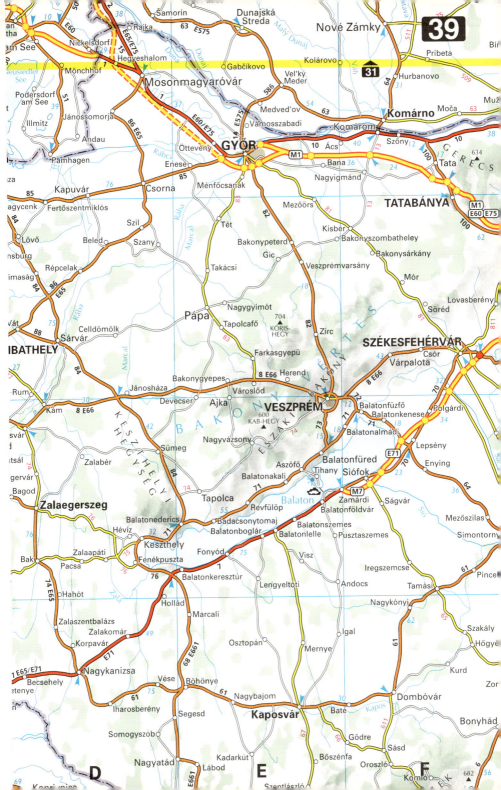

A

Aabenraa DK 2 C3
Aachen D 12 B1
Aalburg NL 12 A3
Aalen D 26 C3
Aalsmeer NL 6 A1
Aalten NL 13 D3
Aarau CH 33 E4
Aarberg CH 33 D3
Aarburg CH 33 E4
Aarschot B 12 A2
Abbekås S 5 D3
Abenberg D 27 E4
Abensberg D 28 A3
Abondance F 32 C2
Abreschviller F 25 D3
Abtenau A 36 C4
Abtshagen D 10 C4
Achenkirch A 35 F4
Achern D 25 F3
Achim D 8 B2
Ács H 39 F4
Adelboden CH 33 D2
Adelebsen D 14 C2
Adelsheim D 20 B1
Adelsried D 27 D2
Adenau D 19 D4
Admont A 37 E4
Adorf D 22 A3
Ærøskobing DK 3 E2
Aerzen D 14 B3
Aflenz A 38 A3
Aggsbach-Dorf A 30 A2
Aggsbach-Markt A 30 A2
Agordo I 36 A1
Ahaus D 13 D4
Ahlbeck D 11 E3
Ahlbeck D 11 E3
Ahlen D 13 E3
Ahlhorn D 8 A2
Ahrensbök D 9 E4
Ahrensburg D 9 D3
Ahrweiler D 19 D4
Åhus S 5 E4
Aicha D 28 C3
Aichach D 27 E2
Aidenbach D 28 C2
Aigen A 29 D2
Aigle CH 32 C2
Aiglsbach D 27 F3
Airolo CH 33 F2
Aïssey F 32 B4
Aiterhofen D 28 B3
Aitrach D 26 C1
Aix-les-Bains F 32 A1
Ajka H 39 E2
Aken D 16 A3
Åkirkeby DK 5 F2
Alagna-Valsésia I 33 D1
Albens F 32 A1
Albersdorf D 2 C1
Albertville F 32 B1
Aldenhoven D 12 C1
Alf D 19 D3
Alfeld D 14 C3
Alfeld D 21 E1
Alkmaar NL 6 A2
Alkoven A 29 E2
Alland A 30 B1
Álleghe I 36 A1
Allensbach D 26 B1
Allersberg D 27 E4
Allershausen D 27 F2
Allinge DK 5 E3
Allstedt D 15 E2
Almelo NL 7 D1
Almere NL 6 B1
Alpbach A 36 A3
Alpen D 12 C3
Alphen-aan den Rijn NL 6 A1

Alpirsbach D 25 F2
Alsenz D 19 E2
Alsfeld D 20 B4
Alsleben D 15 F2
Alstätte D 13 D4
Alt Schadow D 17 D3
Altaussee A 37 D4
Altdorf CH 33 F3
Altdorf D 21 E1
Altena D 13 E2
Altenahr D 19 D4
Altenau D 15 D3
Altenberg D 23 D4
Altenberge D 13 E4
Altenburg D 22 B4
Altenglan D 19 D2
Altenhundem D 13 F1
Altenkirchen D 19 E4
Altenkirchen D 4 C2
Altenmarkt A 37 E4
Altenmarkt D 28 B1
Altenmarkt im Pongau A 36 C3
Altenstadt D 26 C2
Altensteig D 26 A3
Altentreptow D 10 C3
Altenwalde D 8 B4
Altheim A 28 C2
Altkirch F 25 D1
Altmünster A 29 D1
Altötting D 28 B2
Altruppin D 10 B1
Altshausen D 26 B1
Altstätten CH 34 B4
Alzenau D 20 B3
Alzey D 19 E2
Amance F 24 B2
Amancey F 32 B3
Amay B 12 A1
Amberg D 21 F1
Amelinghausen D 9 D2
Amerongen NL 12 B4
Amersfoort NL 12 B4
Amorbach D 20 B2
Ampezzo I 36 B1
Ampfing D 28 B2
Amphion F 32 B2
Amriswil CH 34 B4
Amsteg CH 33 F2
Amsterdam NL 6 A1
Amstetten A 29 F1
Ancerville F 24 A4
Andalo I 35 D1
Andau A 39 D4
Andelot F 24 A3
Andenne B 18 A4
Andermatt CH 33 F2
Andernach D 19 D4
Anderslov S 4 C3
Andijk NL 6 B2
Andocs H 39 E2
Andolsheim F 25 D2
Anger A 38 B3
Angermünde D 11 D2
Angern A 31 D2
Anjum NL 6 C3
Anklam D 11 D3
Ankum D 7 F1
Anna Paulowna NL 6 A2
Annaberg D 36 C3
Annaberg A 38 A4
Annaberg-Buchholz D 22 B3
Annecy F 32 A1
Annemasse F 32 B2
Annenheim A 37 D2
Annweiler D 19 E1
Ansbach D 27 D4
Anterselva/Antholz A 36 A2
Antholz/Anterselva I 36 A2
Apeldoorn NL 12 C4
Apen D 7 F3
Apensen D 8 C3
Apolda D 15 E1
Appelhülsen D 13 E3
Appenweier D 25 E3

Appenzell CH 34 B3
Appiano/Eppan I 35 E1
Appingedam NL 7 D3
Aprica I 34 C1
Arabba I 35 F1
Arbesbach A 29 F2
Arbois F 32 A3
Arbon CH 34 B4
Arcen NL 12 C3
Arches F 24 C2
Ardez CH 34 C2
Arendonk B 12 A2
Arendsee D 9 F1
Argancy F 18 B1
Argegno I 34 A1
Argentière F 32 C1
Arinthod F 32 A2
Arlon B 18 B2
Arneburg D 10 A1
Arnhem NL 12 C4
Arnoldstein A 37 D1
Arnsberg D 13 F2
Arnschwang D 28 C4
Arnstadt D 21 E4
Arnstein D 20 C2
Arolla CH 33 D1
Arolsen D 14 B2
Arosa CH 34 B2
Årøsund DK 3 D3
Arracourt F 24 C3
Årre DK 2 B4
Ars-sur-Moselle F 18 B1
Årslev DK 3 E3
Artemare F 32 A1
Artern D 15 E2
Arth CH 33 F3
Arth D 28 A2
Årup DK 3 D3
Arzberg D 22 A2
Arzl A 35 D3
As B 12 B2
As CZ 22 A3
Ascha D 28 B3
Aschach A 29 D2
Aschaffenburg D 20 B2
Aschau D 36 B4
Aschbach Markt A 29 F1
Ascheberg D 13 E3
Ascheberg D 3 D1
Aschendorf D 7 E2
Aschersleben D 15 F2
Ascona CH 33 F1
Asendorf D 8 B1
Aspang Markt A 38 B3
Assen NL 7 D2
Assens DK 3 D3
Assling D 28 A1
Assmannshausen D 19 E3
Asten A 29 E2
Asten NL 12 B1
Aszófő H 39 E2
Attel D 28 A1
Attendorn D 13 E2
Attersee A 29 D1
Attnang-Puchheim A 29 D1
Atzendorf D 15 F3
Au A 38 A3
Au D 27 F2
Aubange B 18 B2
Auboué F 18 B1
Audeux F 32 B4
Audincourt F 24 C1
Audun-le-Roman F 18 B2
Aue D 22 B3
Auer/Ora I 35 E1
Auerbach D 21 E1
Auerbach D 22 A3
Auffach A 36 A3
Augsburg D 27 E2
Augustenborg DK 3 D3
Augustusburg D 22 C4
Auma D 21 F3
Aumetz F 18 B2
Aurach A 36 B3

Aurach D 27 D4
Aurich D 7 E3
Auronzo di Cadore I 36 B2
Aussernbrünst D 29 D3
Auxonne F 32 A4
Avenches CH 32 C3
Avoriaz F 32 C2
Ayas I 33 D1

B

Baad A 34 C3
Baar D 27 E3
Baarle Nassau NL 12 A3
Baarn NL 6 B1
Babenhausen D 20 A2
Babenhausen D 27 D2
Babigoszcz PL 11 E3
Babylon CZ 28 C4
Baccarat F 24 C3
Bacharach D 19 E3
Backnang D 26 B4
Baczyna PL 11 F1
Bad Abbach D 28 A3
Bad Aibling D 28 A1
Bad Aussee A 37 D4
Bad Bentheim D 13 E4
Bad Bergzabern D 25 F4
Bad Berka D 21 E4
Bad Berleburg D 13 F1
Bad Berneck D 21 F2
Bad Bertrich D 19 D3
Bad Bevensen D 9 D2
Bad Bibra D 15 F1
Bad Blankenburg D 21 E4
Bad Brambach D 22 A3
Bad Bramstedt D 9 D4
Bad Breisig D 19 D4
Bad Brückenau D 20 C3
Bad Buchau D 26 C2
Bad Doberan D 10 A4
Bad Driburg D 14 B3
Bad Düben D 16 B2
Bad Dürkheim D 19 E1
Bad Dürrenberg D 16 A1
Bad Dürrheim D 25 F2
Bad Elster D 22 A3
Bad Ems D 19 E3
Bad Essen D 14 A4
Bad Frankenhausen D 15 E2
Bad Freienwalde D 11 D1
Bad Friedrichshall D 26 B4
Bad Gandersheim D 14 C3
Bad Gleichenberg A 38 B2
Bad Godesberg D 19 D4
Bad Goisern A 37 D4
Bad Gottleuba D 23 D4
Bad Grund D 15 D3
Bad Hall A 29 E1
Bad Harzburg D 15 D3
Bad Herrenalb D 25 F3
Bad Hersfeld D 20 C4
Bad Hofgastein A 36 C3
Bad Homburg D 19 F3
Bad Honnef D 19 D4
Bad Hönnigen D 19 D4
Bad Iburg D 13 F4
Bad Ischl A 37 D4
Bad Kissingen D 20 C3
Bad Kleinen D 9 F3
Bad Kleinkirchheim A 37 D2
Bad König D 20 A2
Bad Königshofen D 21 D3
Bad Kösen D 15 F1
Bad Kreuznach D 19 E2
Bad Krozingen D 25 E2
Bad Langensalza D 15 D1
Bad Lauchstädt D 15 F2
Bad Lausick D 16 B1
Bad Lauterburg D 15 D2
Bad Leonfelden A 29 E2

40

Bad Liebenstein D	21 D4	Bad Salzuflen D	14 B3	Badgastein A	36 C3	Ballerup DK	4 B4
Bad Liebenwerda D	16 C2	Bad Salzungen D	20 C4	Badonviller F	25 D3	Ballum DK	2 B3
Bad Liebenzell D	26 A3	Bad Schallerbach A	29 D2	Bagenkop DK	3 E2	Balmúccia I	33 E1
Bad Lippspringe D	14 B3	Bad Schandau D	23 D4	Bagni del Másino I	34 B1	Balsthal CH	33 E4
Bad Marienberg D	19 E4	Bad Schmiedeberg D	16 B2	Bâgo DK	3 D3	Baltrum D	7 E4
Bad Meinberg D	14 B3	Bad Schönau A	38 C3	Bagod H	39 D2	Bamberg D	21 D2
Bad Mergentheim D	20 B1	Bad Schönborn D	26 A4	Baiersbronn D	25 F3	Bana H	39 E4
Bad Mitterndorf A	37 D4	Bad Schussenried D	26 C2	Bains-les-Bains F	24 B2	Bandholm DK	3 F2
Bad Münder D	14 C4	Bad Schwalbach D	19 E3	Bájánsenye H	38 C2	Banie PL	11 E2
Bad Münster		Bad Schwartau D	9 E4	Bak H	39 D2	Banka SK	31 E2
Ebernburg D	19 E2	Bad Segeberg D	9 D4	Bække DK	2 C4	Bánov CZ	31 E3
Bad Münstereifel D	18 C4	Bad Sooden-Allendorf D	14 C2	Bakonygyepes H	39 E3	Bánovce nad	
Bad Muskau D	17 E2	Bad Sülze D	10 B4	Bakonypeterd H	39 E3	Bebravou SK	31 F3
Bad Nauheim D	20 A3	Bad Tennstedt D	15 D1	Bakonysárkány H	39 F3	Bansin D	11 D4
Bad Nenndorf D	14 C4	Bad Tölz D	35 F4	Bakonyszombatheley H	39 E3	Bar-le-Duc F	24 A4
Bad Neuenahr D	19 D4	Bad Urach D	26 B3	Balatonakali H	39 E2	Barbing D	28 B3
Bad Neustadt D	20 C3	Bad Vöslau A	30 C1	Balatonalmádi H	39 F2	Barchfeld D	21 D4
Bad Oeynhausen D	14 B4	Bad Waldsee D	26 C1	Balatonboglár H	39 E2	Bárcis I	36 B1
Bad Oldesloe D	9 D3	Bad Wiessee D	35 F4	Balatonederics H	39 E2	Bardowick D	9 D2
Bad Orb D	20 B3	Bad Wilsnack D	10 A2	Balatonföldvár H	39 E2	Barenburg D	8 B1
Bad Peterstal D	25 F3	Bad Wimpfen D	26 B4	Balatonfüred H	39 E2	Bargteheide D	9 D3
Bad Pyrmont D	14 B3	Bad Windsheim D	20 C1	Balatonfüzfö H	39 F2	Barlinek PL	11 F1
Bad Ragaz CH	34 B3	Bad Wörishofen D	27 D1	Balatonkenese H	39 F2	Barmstedt D	8 C3
Bad Reichenhall D	36 B4	Bad Wurzach D	26 C1	Balatonkeresztúr H	39 E2	Bärnau D	22 A2
Bad Rippoldsau D	25 F3	Bad Zwischenahn D	7 F2	Balatonlelle H	39 E2	Barneberg D	15 E3
Bad Rothenfelde D	13 F4	Bad-Wildungen D	14 B1	Balatonszemes H	39 E2	Barneveld NL	12 B4
Bad Saarow-Pieskow D	17 D3	Badacsonytomaj H	39 E2	Balderschwang D	34 C4	Barnewitz D	16 B4
Bad Sachsa D	15 D2	Baden A	30 C1	Balingen D	26 A2	Barnstorf D	8 A1
Bad Säckingen D	25 E1	Baden CH	33 E4	Ballebro DK	3 D3	Barntrup D	14 B3
Bad St. Leonhard A	37 F2	Baden-Baden D	25 F3	Ballen DK	3 E4	Barr F	25 D3
Bad Salzdetfurth D	14 C3	Badenweiler D	25 E1	Ballenstedt D	15 E2	Barssel D	7 F2

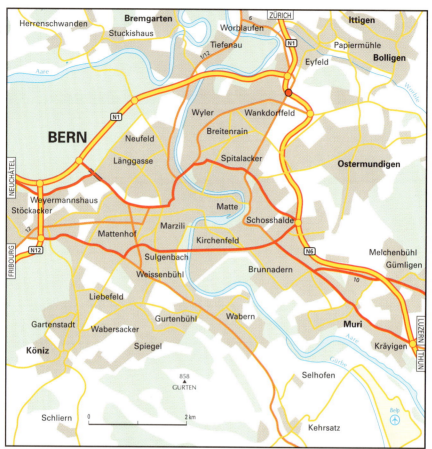

BERN

Barth D	4	B1
Baruth D	16	C3
Barver D	8	A1
Barzio I	34	B1
Basdahl D	8	B3
Basel CH	25	D1
Bassum D	8	B2
Bastogne B	18	B3
Baté H	39	F1
Batelov CZ	30	A4
Battenberg D	14	A1
Battice B	12	B1
Baume-les-Dames F	32	B4
Baumholder D	19	D2
Bautzen D	17	E1
Baveno I	33	E1
Bavorov CZ	29	E3
Bayerisch Eisenstein D	28	C3
Bayon F	24	C3
Bayreuth D	21	E2
Bayrischzell D	36	A4
Beaufort sur Doron F	32	B1
Beaurepaire-en-Bresse F	32	A3
Bebra D	14	C1
Bechhofen D	27	D4
Bechyně CZ	29	E4
Beckenried CH	33	F3
Beckum D	13	E2
Beckum D	13	F3
Becov nad Teplou CZ	22	B2
Becsehely H	39	D1

Beddingestrand S	5	D3
Bederkesa D	8	B3
Beek NL	12	B2
Beek en Donk NL	12	B3
Beelitz D	16	C3
Beerfelden D	20	A2
Beeskow D	17	D3
Beesten D	7	E1
Behringersmühle D	21	E2
Beilen NL	7	D2
Beilngries D	27	F3
Bělá pod Bezdězem CZ	23	E3
Belecke D	13	F2
Beled H	39	D3
Belfort F	24	C1
Belgern D	16	C2
Belgirate I	33	F1
Bellágio I	34	A1
Bellano I	34	B1
Bellegarde-sur-Valserine F	32	A2
Belley F	32	A1
Bellinge DK	3	E3
Bellinzona CH	34	A1
Belluno I	36	A1
Bělotin CZ	31	E4
Belsen (Hohne) D	8	C1
Beltinci SLO	38	C1
Beluša SK	31	F3
Belzig D	16	B3
Benatský nad Jizerou CZ	23	E2

Benediktbeuern D	35	E4
Benešov CZ	23	E1
Benešov nad Ploučnici CZ	23	D3
Benfeld F	25	E3
Benneckenstein D	15	D2
Bennstedt D	15	F2
Bensberg D	13	D1
Bensersiel D	7	F4
Bensheim D	19	F2
Berching D	27	F4
Berchtesgaden D	36	C4
Berg D	27	E1
Berg-Neustadt D	13	E1
Berga D	15	E2
Bergedorf D	9	D3
Bergen D	9	D1
Bergen D	9	E2
Bergen D	4	C1
Bergen NL	6	A2
Bergen aan Zee NL	6	A2
Bergheim D	12	C1
Bergisch Gladbach D	13	D1
Berglern D	28	A2
Bergum NL	6	C3
Bergün CH	34	B2
Beringen B	12	A2
Berkenthin D	9	E3
Berkheim D	26	C2
Berkhof D	8	C1
Berlin D	16	C4

Berlingen CH	26	B1
Bern CH	33	D3
Bernartice CZ	29	E4
Bernau D	36	B4
Bernau D	11	D1
Bernburg D	15	F2
Berndorf A	30	B1
Berne D	8	A2
Bernhardsthal A	31	D2
Bernkastel-Kues D	19	D3
Bernsdorf D	17	D1
Bernstein A	38	C3
Beromünster CH	33	E3
Beroun CZ	23	D2
Bersenbrück D	7	F1
Bertrix B	18	A3
Berwang A	35	D3
Besançon F	32	B4
Besigheim D	26	B4
Betzdorf D	13	E1
Beuel D	13	D1
Beuron D	26	B2
Beverstedt D	8	B3
Beverungen D	14	B2
Beverwijk NL	6	A2
Bex CH	32	C2
Bezau A	34	C4
Biasca CH	34	A2
Biberach D	25	E2
Biberach an der Riss D	26	C2
Bichl D	35	E4

Bieber D 20 B3
Biebersdorf D 17 D3
Biedenkopf D 14 A1
Biel/Bienne CH 33 D3
Bielefeld D 14 A3
Bienenbüttel D 9 D2
Bienne/Biel CH 33 D3
Biesenthal D 11 D1
Bietigheim D 26 B4
Bignasco CH 33 F1
Bilina CZ 23 D3
Billerbeck D 13 E3
Billund DK 2 C4
Bingen D 19 E2
Binz D 5 D1
Birkenfeld D 19 D2
Birkenwerder D 10 C1
Birkerød DK 4 B4
Birkfeld A 38 B3
Birnau D 26 B1
Bischofsgrün D 21 F2
Bischofsheim D 20 C3
Bischofshofen A 36 C3
Bischofswerda D 17 D1
Bismark D 9 F1
Bispingen D 9 D2
Bitburg D 18 C3
Bitche F 25 E4
Bitov CZ 30 B3
Bitterfeld D 16 B2
Blâmont F 25 D3
Blankenburg D 15 E3
Blankenfelde D 16 C3
Blankenhain D 21 E4
Blankenheim D 18 C4
Blansko CZ 30 C4
Blatná CZ 29 D4
Blatnice CZ 31 E3
Blaubeuren D 26 C2
Blaufelden D 20 C1
Blaustein D 26 C2
Blåvand DK 2 B4
Bleckede D 9 E2
Bled SLO 37 D1
Bleiburg A 37 F1
Bleicherode D 15 D2
Bletterans F 32 A3
Blexen D 8 B3
Blieskastel D 19 D1
Blokzijl NL 6 C2
Blomberg D 14 B3
Blovice CZ 22 C1
Bludenz A 34 C3
Blumberg D 25 F1
Bobingen D 27 E2
Bobitz D 9 F3
Böblingen D 26 B3
Bobrowice PL 17 F3
Bocholt D 13 D3
Bochov CZ 22 B2
Bochum D 13 D2
Bockel D 8 C2
Bockenem D 15 D3
Böckstein A 36 C3
Bockum-Hovel D 13 E3
Bodegraven NL 12 A4
Bodenmais D 28 C3
Bodenteich D 9 E1
Bodenwerder D 14 C3
Bodenwöhr D 28 B4
Bodman D 26 B1
Boëge F 32 B2
Bogatynia PL 23 E4
Bogdaniec PL 17 F4
Bogen D 28 B3
Bogense DK 3 D4
Bohdalov CZ 30 B4
Bohinjska Bistrica SLO 37 D1
Böhmenkirch D 26 C3
Bohmte D 14 A4
Böhönye H 39 E1
Boitzenburg D 11 D2
Boizenburg D 9 E3
Bøjden DK 3 D3

Bolemin PL 17 F4
Boleshawiec PL 17 E1
Boleszkowice PL 11 E1
Bologne F 24 A3
Bulsward NL 6 B3
Boltenhagen D 9 F4
Boltigen CH 33 D2
Bolzano/Bozen I 35 E2
Bonaduz CH 34 B2
Bonlieu F 32 A3
Bonn D 13 D1
Bonndorf D 25 F1
Bonneville F 32 B1
Bonyhád H 39 F1
Bopfingen D 27 D3
Boppard D 19 E3
Bor CZ 22 B1
Borchen D 14 A3
Borculo NL 13 D4
Bordesholm D 3 D1
Borgentreich D 14 B2
Börger D 7 E2
Borger NL 7 D2
Borgholzhausen D 14 A4
Borghorst D 13 E4
Borgo Valsugana I 35 E1
Borken D 13 D3
Borken D 14 B1
Børkop DK 3 D4
Borkum D 7 D4
Bórmio I 34 C2
Borna D 16 B1
Bornhöved D 9 D4
Börnicke D 10 C1
Borovany CZ 29 E3
Borrby S 5 E3
Borre DK 4 B2
Borup DK 4 B4
Boskoop NL 12 A4
Boskovice CZ 30 C4
Bószénfa H 39 E1
Bottrop D 13 D3
Boudry CH 32 C3
Bouillon B 18 A3
Boulay-Moselle F 18 C1
Bourbonne-les-Bains F 24 B2
Bourmont F 24 A3
Bouxwiller F 25 E4
Bouzonville F 18 C1
Bovec SLO 36 C1
Bovrup DK 2 C3
Bovtoft DK 2 C3
Boxberg D 20 B1
Boxmeer NL 12 C3
Boxtel NL 12 B3
Bozen/Bolzano I 35 E2
Brackenheim D 26 B4
Brackwede D 14 A3
Brake D 8 A3
Brakel D 14 B3
Bramming DK 2 B4
Bramsche D 7 F1
Brand A 34 C3
Brand-Erbisdorf D 22 C4
Brandenberg A 36 A4
Brandenburg D 16 B4
Brandis D 16 C2
Brandýs n Labem CZ 23 E2
Brandýsek CZ 23 D2
Branišovice CZ 30 C3
Brankovice CZ 31 D3
Brannenburg D 36 A4
Branzi I 34 B1
Bratislava SK 31 D1
Braubach D 19 E3
Braunau A 28 C2
Braunfels D 19 F4
Braunlage D 15 D2
Braunschweig D 15 D4
Břeclav CZ 31 D3
Breda NL 12 A3
Bredebro DK 2 B3
Bredelar D 14 A2
Bredstedt D 2 C2

Bree B 12 B2
Bregenz A 34 C4
Brehna D 16 A2
Breisach D 25 E2
Breisen D 10 B1
Breitengussbach
  Hallstadt D 21 D2
Bremen D 8 B2
Bremerhaven D 8 B3
Bremervörde D 8 C3
Bressanone/Brixen I 35 F2
Bretten D 26 A4
Breuil-Cervinia I 33 D1
Breuna D 14 B2
Březnice CZ 23 D1
Brezová SK 31 E2
Brienz CH 33 E3
Brieskow-Finkenheerd D ... 17 E3
Briey F 18 B1
Brig CH 33 E2
Brilon D 14 A2
Brinkum D 8 B2
Brissago CH 33 F1
Brixen/Bressanone I 35 F2
Brixlegg A 35 E1
Brněnec CZ 30 C4
Brno CZ 30 C3
Broager DK 3 D2
Bröckel D 15 D4
Brodenbach D 19 D3
Brody PL 17 E2
Brody PL 17 F3
Brohl D 19 D4
Brome D 9 E1
Brøns DK 2 B3
Brørup DK 2 C4
Brösarp S 5 E4
Brouvelieures F 24 C2
Brtnice CZ 30 B4
Bruchhausen-Vilsen D 8 B2
Bruchsal D 26 A4
Bruck D 28 B4
Bruck D 16 B3
Bruck an der Grossglock-
  nerstrasse A 36 B3
Bruck an der Leitha A 31 D1
Bruck an der Mur A 38 A3
Brückl A 37 E2
Brüel D 10 A3
Brugg CH 33 E4
Brühl D 13 D1
Brumath F 25 E3
Brummen NL 12 C4
Brunau D 9 F1
Bruneck/Brunico I 35 F2
Brunico/Bruneck I 35 F2
Brunnen CH 33 F3
Brunnen CH 33 F3
Brunsbüttel D 8 C4
Brunssum NL 12 B1
Brüssow D 11 D2
Bruyères F 24 C2
Bučany SK 31 E2
Buchen D 20 B1
Buchen D 9 E3
Buchenwald D 15 E1
Buchholz D 9 D3
Buchloe D 27 D1
Buchs CH 34 B3
Bückeburg D 14 B4
Bücken D 8 B1
Buckow D 17 D4
Büdingen D 20 B3
Budyně nad Ohří CZ 23 D3
Bühl D 25 F3
Buitenpost NL 6 C3
Bülach CH 33 F4
Bulgnéville F 24 B3
Bulle CH 32 C2
Bunde D 7 E3
Bünde D 14 A4
Burbach D 19 E4
Büren CH 33 D3
Büren D 14 A2

Burg D 3 F1
Burg D 16 A3
Burg Stargard D 10 C3
Burg Vetschau D 17 D2
Burgau D 27 D2
Burgbernheim D 20 C1
Burgdorf CH 33 D3
Burgdorf D 15 D4
Burgebrach D 21 D2
Bürgel D 21 F4
Burghaun D 20 C4
Burghausen D 28 B2
Burgjoss D 20 B3
Burgkunstadt D 21 E2
Burglengenfeld D 28 A4
Burgsinn D 20 B3
Burgsteinfurt D 13 E4
Burladingen D 26 B2
Bürstadt D 19 F2
Busdorf D 2 C2
Bussang F 24 C2
Bussum NL 6 B1
Büsum D 2 B1
Bütgenbach B 18 C4
Buttelstedt D 15 E1
Buttstädt D 15 E1
Butzbach D 20 A3
Bützow D 10 A3
Buxtehude D 8 C3
Bylnice CZ 31 E3
Bystřice CZ 23 E1
Bystřice nad
  Pernštejnem CZ 30 C4
Bystřice pod
  Hostýnem CZ 31 E4
Bytča SK 31 F4
Bzenec CZ 31 D3

C

Cadenábbia I 34 A1
Cadenberge D 8 B4
Čakajovce SK 31 F2
Cakovec HR 38 C1
Calau D 17 D2
Calbe D 15 F3
Calvörde D 15 E4
Calw D 26 A3
Camberg D 19 F3
Camburg D 15 F1
Campo Tures/
  Sand in Taufers I 35 F2
Campocologno CH 34 C1
Canazei I 35 F1
Cánnero Riviera I 33 F1
Cannóbio I 33 F1
Capo di Ponte I 34 C1
Carbonin/Schludersbach I ... 36 A2
Carignan F 18 A2
Carling F 18 C1
Carlow D 9 E3
Carnia I 36 C1
Carolinensiel D 7 F4
Casekow D 11 D2
Čáslav CZ 23 E1
Castricum NL 6 A2
Castrop-Rauxal D 13 E3
Cavalese I 35 E1
Čechtice CZ 23 E1
Cedynia PL 11 D1
Čejč CZ 31 D3
Čelákovice CZ 23 E2
Celerina CH 34 C2
Celje SLO 38 A1
Celldömölk H 39 D3
Celle D 9 D1
Cencenighe I 35 F1
Černá I 29 E3
Černá Hora CZ 30 C4
Cernay F 25 D1
Černošín CZ 22 B2

Černovice CZ 29 F4
Červená-Řečice CZ ...... 23 FI
Česká Kamenice CZ 23 E4
Česká Lipa CZ 23 E3
České Budějovice CZ 29 E3
České Velenice CZ 29 F3
Český Brod CZ 23 E2
Český Krumlov CZ 29 E3
Chalampé F .... 25 DI
Cham CH 33 F3
Cham D 28 B4
Chambley-Bussières F ...... 18 BI
Chamonix-Mont-Blanc F .. 32 CI
Champagnole F 32 A3
Champéry CH 32 C2
Champex CH .... 32 CI
Champlitte F .... 24 AI
Champlon B 18 A3
Champoluc I .... 33 DI
Charmes F 24 C3
Chassigny F 24 A2
Château d'Oex CH 32 C2
Château-Salins F 24 C4
Châtel F 32 C2
Châtel-St-Denis CH 32 C2
Châtenois F 24 B3
Chaumergy F 32 A3
Chaumont F 24 A3
Chaussin F 32 A3
Cheb CZ 22 A2
Chemnitz D 22 B4
Chieming D .... 28 FI
Chiesa in Valmalenco I .. 34 BI
Chiusa/Klausen I 35 E2
Chiusaforte I .... 36 CI
Chlebowo PL 17 E3
Chlumec nad
  Cidlinou CZ 23 F2
Chociwel PL 11 F2
Chodová Planá CZ 22 B2
Chojna PL .... 11 EI
Chomutov CZ 22 C3
Choszczno PL 11 F2
Chotěboř CZ .... 23 FI
Choye F .... 24 AI
Chrastava CZ 23 E4
Christiansfeld DK 2 C3
Chur CH 34 B2
Chyňava CZ 23 D2
Chýnov CZ 29 F4
Ciney B 18 A4
Cinovec CZ 23 D3
Cirey F 25 D3
Clairvaux-les-Lacs F 32 A3
Clausthal-Zellerfeld D .. 15 D3
Clefmont F 24 A2
Clerval D 32 C4
Clervaux L 18 B3
Cles I .... 35 EI
Cloppenburg D 7 F2
Cluses F .... 32 BI
Coburg D 21 E3
Cochem D 19 D3
Coesfeld D 13 D3
Coevorden NL 7 D2
Cölbe D .... 14 AI
Colbitz D 15 F4
Colditz D .... 16 BI
Colico I .... 34 BI
Colle Isarco/Gossensass I .. 35 E2
Collonges F 32 A2
Colmar F 25 D2
Colombey-les-Belles F .. 24 B3
Combeaufontaine F 24 B2
Commercy F 24 B4
Conflans F .... 18 BI
Contrexéville F 24 B3
Coppenbrügge D 14 C3
Corcieux F 25 D2
Cornimont F 24 C2
Cortina d'Ampezzo I .. 36 A2
Corvara in Badia I 35 F2
Cossonay CH 32 B3

Coswig D 16 B3
Cottbus D 17 E2
Courmayeur I .... 32 CI
Couvet CH 32 C3
Crailsheim D 27 D4
Crans CH 33 D2
Creglingen D .... 20 CI
Cresta CH 34 B2
Creussen D 21 E2
Creutzwald F .... 18 CI
Creuzburg D .... 15 DI
Crimmitschau D 22 A4
Crivitz D 9 F3
Črna SLO .... 37 FI
Cruseilles F .... 32 AI
Csór H 39 F3
Csorna H 39 D4
Cuijk NL 12 B3
Culemborg NL 12 B4
Culoz F .... 32 AI
Cuxhaven D 8 B4
Cvikov CZ 23 E3
Cybinka PL 17 E3

D

Dąbie PL 11 E2
Dabo F 25 D3
Dachau D 27 E2
Dačice CZ 30 A3
Dahlen D .... 16 BI
Dahlenburg D 9 E2
Dahme D .... 3 EI
Dahme D 16 C2
Dahmen D 10 B3
Dahn D 25 E4
Dalby S 5 D4
Damme D .... 8 AI
Damp 2000 D 3 D2
Dampierre F 32 A4
Dampierre-sur-Salon F .. 24 AI
Damvillers F 18 A2
Dannemarie F .... 25 DI
Dannenberg D 9 E2
Dardesheim D 15 E3
Dargun D 10 C3
Därligen CH 33 D2
Darmstadt D 19 F2
Darney F 24 B2
Dasburg D 18 B3
Dasing D 27 E2
Dassel D 14 C3
Dassow D 9 E4
Dasswang D 27 F4
Datteln D 13 E3
Daun D 18 C3
Davle CZ 23 D2
Davos CH 34 C2
De Cocksdorp NL 6 B3
De Koog NL 6 A3
De Kooy NL 6 A2
Dębno PL .... 11 EI
Děčín CZ 23 D4
Dedemsvaart NL 7 D2
Degebüll D 2 B2
Degerndorf D 36 A4
Deggendorf D 28 C3
Deidesheim D .... 19 EI
Delbrück D 14 A3
Delden NL 13 D4
Delémont CH 33 D4
Delfzijl NL 7 E3
Delitzsch D 16 B2
Delle F .... 24 CI
Delme F 24 C4
Delmenhorst D 8 B2
Demmin D 10 C3
Den Burg NL 6 A3
Den Helder NL 6 A3
Den Oever NL 6 B2
Denekamp NL .... 7 DI

Denkendorf D 27 F3
Denzlingen D 25 E2
Dermbach D 20 C4
Derneburg D 15 D3
Dešov CZ 30 B3
Detmold D 14 B3
Dettelbach D 20 C2
Deurne NL 12 B3
Deutsch-Wagram A .. 30 C2
Deutschkreutz A 38 C4
Deutschlandsberg A .. 38 A2
Devecser H 39 E2
Deventer NL .... 6 CI
Dianalund DK 4 A4
Dieburg D 20 A2
Diekirch L 18 B3
Diemelstadt D 14 B2
Dienten A 36 C3
Diepholz D .... 8 AI
Dierdorf D 19 E4
Dieren NL 12 C4
Diesdorf D .... 9 EI
Diessen D .... 27 EI
Diest B 12 A2
Dietenheim D 26 C2
Dietfurt D 27 F3
Dietikon CH 33 F4
Dietmannsried D ...... 27 DI
Dieulouard F 24 B4
Dieuze F 24 C4
Diever NL 6 C2
Diez D 19 E3
Differdange L 18 B2
Dignano I .... 36 BI
Dillenburg D 19 F4
Dillingen D .... 18 CI
Dillingen D 27 D3
Dimaro I .... 35 DI
Dingelstädt D 15 D2
Dingolfing D 28 B3
Dinkelsbühl D 27 D4
Dinklage D .... 7 FI
Dinozé F 24 C2
Dinslaken D 13 D3
Dippoldiswalde D 22 C4
Disentis/Mustér CH .. 34 A2
Ditzingen D 26 B3
Divonne F 32 B2
Dobbiaco/Toblach I .. 36 A2
Dobel D 26 A3
Döbeln D .... 16 CI
Doberlug Kirchhain D .. 16 C2
Döbern D 17 E2
Dobersberg A 30 A3
Dobra PL 11 F3
Döbriach A 37 D2
Dobřichovice CZ 23 D2
Dobříš CZ .... 23 DI
Dobrzany PL 11 F2
Doesburg NL 12 C4
Doetinchem NL 12 C4
Dokkum NL 6 C3
Doksy CZ 23 E3
Dole F 32 A4
Dolga Vas SLO .... 38 CI
Dolice NL 11 F2
Döllach A 36 B2
Döllbach D 20 C3
Dolle D 15 F4
Döllstädt D .... 15 DI
Dolni Dvonste CZ 29 E2
Domažlice CZ 28 C4
Dombasle F 24 C3
Dombóvár H .... 39 FI
Dombrot-le-Sec F 24 B2
Domève-en-Haye F .. 24 B4
Dömitz D 9 E2
Dommitzsch D 16 B2
Domodóssola I .... 33 EI
Dompaire F 24 B3
Domrémy-la-Pucelle F .. 24 B3
Domzale SLO .... 37 EI
Donaueschingen D .. 25 F2
Donaustauf D 28 B3

Donauwörth D 27 E3
Donnersbach A 37 D3
Doorn NL 12 B4
Dordrecht NL 12 A4
Dorfen D 28 A2
Dorfmark D 8 C2
Dormagen D 13 D2
Dornauberg A 35 F3
Dornbirn A 34 C4
Dornburg D 21 F4
Dorndorf D 20 C4
Dornstetten D 26 A3
Dornum D 7 E4
Dörpen D 7 E2
Dörpstedt D 2 C2
Dorsten D 13 D3
Dortan F 32 A2
Dortmund D 13 E2
Dorum D 8 B3
Dörverden D 8 B2
Dörzbach D .... 20 BI
Doucier F 32 A3
Doulaincourt F 24 A3
Douvaine F 32 B2
Drachselsried D 28 C3
Drachten NL 6 C3
Dragør DK 4 C4
Drahonice CZ 29 E4
Drahovce SK 31 E2
Dransfeld D 14 C2
Dranske D 4 C2
Drasenhofen A 30 C3
Dravograd SLO .... 37 FI
Draženov CZ .... 22 BI
Drebkau D 17 D2
Dreilingen D 9 D2
Drensteinfurt D 13 E3
Dresden D 23 D4
Drewitz D 16 A3
Drewitz D 16 C4
Driebergen NL 12 B4
Drnholec CZ 30 C3
Drochtersen D 8 C3
Dronten NL .... 6 CI
Drosendorf Stadt A 30 B3
Drosselbjerg DK 3 F4
Drusenheim F 25 E3
Druten NL 12 B4
Dubá CZ 23 E3
Duben D 17 D3
Dubnica nad Váhom SK .. 31 F3
Ducherow D 11 D3
Dudelange L 18 B2
Duderstadt D 15 D2
Düdingen CH 33 D3
Duingt F .... 32 BI
Duisburg D 13 D2
Dülken D 12 C2
Dülmen D 13 E3
Dun F 18 A2
Dunajská Streda SK .. 31 EI
Durbuy B 18 A4
Düren D .... 12 CI
Dürnkrut A 31 D2
Dürnstein A 30 B2
Düsseldorf D 13 D2
Dwingeloo NL 7 D2
Dziwnów PL 11 E4

E

Ebelsbach D 21 D2
Eben im Pongau A .. 36 C3
Ebenfurth A 38 C4
Ebensee A 37 D4
Eberbach D .... 20 AI
Ebermannstadt D .. 21 E2
Ebern D 21 D2
Ebersbach D 23 E4
Ebersberg D .... 28 AI
Eberschwang A .... 29 DI

Ebersdorf D	8 B3	Emsdetten D	13 E4
Eberstein A	37 E2	Emskirchen D	21 D1
Eberswalde D	11 D1	Emstek D	8 A2
Ebingen D	26 B2	Endorf D	28 B1
Ebrach D	21 D2	Enese H	39 E4
Ebreichsdorf A	30 C1	Engelberg CH	33 F3
Ebstorf D	9 D2	Engelhartszell A	29 D2
Echallens CH	32 C3	Engelskirchen D	13 E1
Echallon F	32 A2	Engen D	26 A1
Echternach L	18 C2	Enger D	14 A4
Eckartsberga D	15 F1	Engstingen D	26 B2
Eckernförde D	3 D2	Enkhuizen NL	6 B2
Ecthe D	14 C3	Enns A	29 E2
Edam NL	6 B2	Enschede NL	13 D4
Ede NL	12 B4	Ensisheim F	25 D2
Edenkoben D	19 E1	Entlebuch CH	33 E3
Edersee D	14 B1	Entrèves I	32 C1
Edewecht D	7 F2	Enying H	39 F2
Édolo I	34 C1	Epe D	13 D4
Eferding A	29 D2	Epe NL	6 C1
Egeln D	15 E3	Épinal F	24 C2
Egernsund DK	3 D2	Eppan/Appiano I	35 E1
Egervár H	39 D2	Eppingen D	26 B4
Egestorf D	9 D2	Erbach D	20 A2
Egg A	34 C4	Erbendorf D	21 F2
Eggenburg A	30 B2	Erding D	28 A2
Eggenfelden D	28 B2	Erfde D	2 C1
Eggesin D	11 D3	Erftstadt D	12 C1
Eghezée B	12 A1	Erfurt D	15 E1
Egmond aan Zee NL	6 A2	Ergoldsbach D	28 B3
Egtved DK	2 C4	Erkelenz D	12 C2
Ehingen D	26 C2	Erlangen D	21 D1
Ehnen L	18 B2	Erlenbach D	20 B2
Ehra-Lessien D	9 E1	Erlsbach A	36 A2
Ehrwald A	35 E3	Ermelo NL	6 B1
Eibenstock D	22 B3	Ermsleben D	15 E2
Eibergen NL	13 D4	Erndtebrück D	13 F1
Eibiswald A	38 A2	Ernstbrunn A	30 C2
Eich D	19 F2	Erstein F	25 E3
Eichendorf D	28 C2	Erwitte D	13 F2
Eichstätt D	27 E3	Erxleben D	15 E3
Eigenrieden D	15 D1	Esbjerg DK	2 B4
Eilenburg D	16 B2	Esch-sur-Alzette L	18 B2
Eilsleben D	15 E3	Esch-sur-Sûre L	18 B3
Einbeck D	14 C3	Eschede D	9 D1
Eindhoven NL	12 B1	Eschenbach D	21 F2
Einsiedeln CH	34 A3	Eschenburg-	
Eisenach D	15 D1	Eibelshausen D	19 F4
Eisenberg D	21 F4	Eschenlohe D	35 E4
Eisenerz A	37 F3	Eschershausen D	14 C3
Eisenhüttenstadt D	17 E3	Eschwege D	14 C1
Eisenkappel A	37 E1	Eschweiler D	12 C1
Eisenstadt A	38 C4	Esens D	7 F4
Eisfeld D	21 D3	Eslohe D	13 F2
Eislingen D	26 C3	Eslöv S	5 D4
Eitorf D	13 D1	Espelkamp D	14 A4
Elbigenalp A	35 D3	Essen D	13 D2
Elbingerode D	15 E3	Essen D	7 F2
Elburg NL	6 C1	Essenbach D	28 B3
Eldena D	9 F2	Esslingen D	26 B3
Elgg CH	34 A4	Estavayer-le-Lac CH	32 C3
Ellenberg D	27 D4	Esterwegen D	7 E2
Ellingen D	27 E4	Étain F	18 A1
Ellrich D	15 D2	Etalle B	18 A2
Ellwangen D	27 D3	Ettelbruck L	18 B3
Elmpt D	12 C2	Ettenheim D	25 E2
Elmshorn D	8 B2	Ettlingen D	25 F4
Elsdorf D	12 C1	Eupen B	12 B1
Elsfleth D	8 A3	Euratsfeld A	29 F1
Elst NL	12 B4	Euskirchen D	18 C4
Elster D	16 B2	Eussenhausen D	21 D3
Elsterberg D	22 A3	Eutin D	9 E4
Elsterwerda D	16 C2	Eutzsch D	16 B2
Elten D	12 C3	Evendorf D	9 D2
Eltmann D	21 D2	Evian F	32 B2
Eltville D	19 E3	Evolène CH	33 D1
Elzach D	25 E2	Extertal D	14 B3
Elze D	14 C3		
Emden D	7 E3		
Emlichheim D	7 D1		
Emmeloord NL	6 C2		
Emmen NL	7 D2		
Emmendingen D	25 E2		
Emmerich D	12 C3	Faak A	37 D1

Fåborg DK	3 D3	Frankenburg A	28 C1
Faido CH	33 F2	Frankenmarkt A	28 C1
Fakse DK	4 B3	Frankenthal D	19 F2
Fakse Ladeplads DK	4 B3	Frankfurt (Oder) D	17 E3
Falcade I	35 F1	Frankfurt am Main D	20 A3
Falkenberg S	16 C2	Františkovy Lázné CZ	22 A2
Falkenstein D	22 A3	Franz Josephs-Höhe A	36 B3
Fallersleben D	15 E4	Franzburg D	10 C4
Fallingbostel D	8 C2	Frasdorf D	36 B4
Falsterbo S	4 C3	Frauenau D	28 C3
Farébersviller F	18 C1	Frauenfeld CH	34 A4
Farkasgyepü H	39 E3	Frauenstein D	22 C4
Farum DK	4 B4	Frechen D	13 D1
Faucogney-et-la-Mer F	24 C2	Freckenhorst D	13 F3
Faulensee CH	33 D2	Fredensborg DK	4 B4
Faulquemont F	24 C4	Fredericia DK	3 D4
Faverges F	32 B1	Frederiksberg DK	4 A3
Faverney F	24 B2	Frederikssund DK	4 B4
Fayl-Billot F	24 A2	Freiberg D	22 C4
Fehrbellin D	10 B1	Freiburg D	8 C4
Fehring A	38 B2	Freiburg im Breisgau D	25 E2
Feld A	37 D2	Freihung D	21 F1
Feldafing D	27 E1	Freilassing D	28 C1
Feldbach A	38 B2	Freising D	27 F2
Feldberg D	25 E1	Freistadt A	29 E2
Feldberg D	10 C2	Freital D	22 C4
Feldkirch A	34 B3	Freren D	7 E1
Feldkirchen A	37 D2	Fresnes F	24 B2
Feldkirchen D	27 F1	Fresnes-en-Woëvre F	18 A1
Feldsted DK	2 C3	Fretigney-et-Velloreille F	24 B1
Fellbach D	26 B3	Fretzdorf D	10 B2
Fenékpuszta H	39 D2	Freudenburg D	13 E1
Fénétrange F	25 D4	Freudenberg D	20 B2
Ferdinandshof D	11 D3	Freudenstadt D	25 F3
Ferleiten A	36 B3	Freyenstein D	10 B2
Ferrette F	33 D4	Freyming	
Fertöszentmiklós H	39 D3	Merlebach F	18 C1
Feucht D	21 E1	Freystadt D	27 E4
Feuchtwangen D	27 D4	Freyung D	29 D3
Fieberbrunn A	36 B3	Fribourg CH	32 C3
Fiera di Primiero I	35 F1	Frick CH	33 E4
Fiesch CH	33 E2	Fridingen D	26 A2
Finnentrop D	13 E2	Friedberg A	38 B3
Finow D	11 D1	Friedberg D	20 A3
Finsterwalde D	17 D2	Friedberg D	27 E2
Fischamend A	30 C1	Friedeburg D	7 F3
Fischbach D	25 E4	Friedersdorf D	17 D3
Fischbeck D	16 A4	Friedewald D	20 C4
Fischen D	34 C4	Friedland D	14 C2
Fladungen D	20 C3	Friedland D	11 D3
Flaine F	32 B1	Friedland D	17 D3
Flavigny-sur-Moselle F	24 C3	Friedrichroda D	21 D4
Flensburg D	2 C2	Friedrichshafen D	34 B4
Fleurier CH	32 C3	Friedrichskoog D	8 B4
Flims Waldhaus CH	34 B2	Friedrichsort D	3 D1
Flöha D	22 C4	Friedrichstadt D	2 C1
Florenville B	18 A2	Friesack A	37 E2
Florstadt D	20 A3	Friesack D	10 B1
Flüelen CH	33 F3	Friesoythe D	7 F2
Flumet F	32 B1	Fritzlar D	14 B1
Flums CH	34 B3	Frohburg D	16 B1
Fockbek D	2 C1	Frohnleiten A	38 A3
Fohnsdorf A	37 E3	Frontenhausen D	28 B2
Foldingbro DK	2 C4	Frutigen CH	33 D2
Folmava CZ	28 C4	Frýdlant CZ	23 F4
Fondo I	35 E1	Frymburk CZ	29 E2
Fontaine-Française F	24 A1	Fügen A	35 F3
Fonyód H	39 E2	Fuglebjerg DK	4 A3
Fóppolo I	34 B1	Fuhrberg D	8 C1
Forbach D	25 F3	Fulda D	20 C3
Forbach F	18 C1	Fulpmes A	35 E3
Forchheim D	21 E2	Fürstenau D	7 E1
Forni di Sopra I	36 B1	Fürstenberg D	10 C2
Forno di Zoldo I	36 A1	Fürstenfeld A	38 B2
Forst D	17 E2	Fürstenfeldbruck D	27 E2
Forth D	21 E1	Fürstenwalde D	17 D4
Fougerolles F	24 C2	Fürstenwerder D	11 D2
Foulain F	24 A2	Fürstenzell D	28 C2
Fraize F	25 D2	Fürth D	21 D1
Frammersbach D	20 B3	Furth im Wald D	28 C4
Franeker NL	6 C3	Furtwangen D	25 F2
Frangy F	32 A1	Fusch A	36 B3
Frankenberg D	14 A1	Füssen D	35 D4
Frankenberg D	22 B4	Fynshav DK	3 D3

G

Gabčíkovo *SK* 39 E4
Gadebusch *D* 9 E3
Gaggenau *D* 25 F3
Gaildorf *D* 26 C4
Gajary *SK* 31 D2
Galanta *SK* 31 E1
Gallneukirchen *A* 29 E2
Galtür *A* 34 C3
Gaming *A* 29 F1
Gammertingen *D* 26 B2
Gams *CH* 34 B3
Ganacker *D* 28 B3
Ganderkesee *D* 8 B2
Gandria *CH* 34 A1
Gangkofen *D* 28 B2
Gänserndorf *A* 30 C2
Garching *D* 28 B1
Gardelegen *D* 15 F4
Garding *D* 2 B1
Gargellen *A* 34 C3
Garlstorf *D* 9 D2
Garmisch
Partenkirchen *D* 35 E4
Garrel *D* 7 F2
Gars am Kamp *A* 30 B2
Garsnas *S* 5 E3
Gartow *D* 9 F2
Gartringen *D* 26 B3
Gartz *D* 11 E2
Garz *D* 4 C1
Gaschurn *A* 34 C3
Gasztony *H* 38 C2
Gebesee *D* 15 E1
Gedem *D* 20 B3
Gedser *DK* 4 A2
Geel *B* 12 A2
Geertruidenberg *NL* 12 A3
Geesthacht *D* 9 D3
Gefell *D* 21 F3
Gefrees *D* 21 F2
Gehren *D* 21 E4
Geilenkirchen *D* 12 C2
Geisa *D* 20 C4
Geiselhöring *D* 28 B3
Geisenfeld *D* 27 F3
Geisenhausen *D* 28 B2
Geisingen *D* 26 A1
Geislingen *D* 26 C3
Geithain *D* 16 B1
Geldern *D* 12 C3
Geldrop *NL* 12 B3
Geleen *NL* 12 B2
Gelnhausen *D* 20 B3
Gelsenkirchen *D* 13 D3
Gelting *D* 3 D2
Gemert *NL* 12 B3
Gemona del Friuli *I* 36 C1
Gemünd *D* 18 C4
Gemünden *D* 19 D2
Gemünden *D* 14 B1
Gemunden *D* 20 C2
Genève *CH* 32 B2
Genk *B* 12 B2
Gennep *NL* 12 C3
Genthin *D* 16 A4
Georgsheil *D* 7 E3
Gera *D* 22 A4
Gerabronn *D* 26 C4
Gérardmer *F* 24 C3
Geras *A* 30 B3
Gerbéviller *F* 24 C3
Gerbstedt *D* 15 F2
Gerchsheim *D* 20 C2
Geretsried *D* 27 E1
Gerlos *A* 36 A3
Germay *F* 24 A3
Germersheim *D* 19 E1
Gernrode *D* 15 E2
Gernsbach *D* 25 F3

Gernsheim *D* 19 F2
Gerolstein *D* 18 C3
Gerolzhofen *D* 20 C2
Gersfeld *D* 20 C3
Gersthofen *D* 27 E2
Gescher *D* 13 D3
Geseke *D* 14 A3
Gettorf *D* 3 D1
Gex *F* 32 B2
Gföhl *A* 30 A2
Gic *H* 39 E3
Gieboldehausen *D* 15 D2
Giengen *D* 27 D3
Gieselwerder *D* 14 C2
Giessen *D* 20 A4
Gieten *NL* 7 D2
Giethoorn *NL* 6 C2
Gifhorn *D* 15 D4
Giornico *CH* 34 A2
Giromagny *F* 24 C1
Gislev *DK* 3 E3
Givry-en-Argonne *F* 24 A4
Gladbeck *D* 13 D3
Gladenbach *D* 20 A4
Glamsbjerg *DK* 3 D3
Glandorf *D* 13 F4
Glarus *CH* 34 A3
Glashütte *D* 23 D4
Glauchau *D* 22 B4
Gleisdorf *A* 38 B3
Gletsch *CH* 33 E2
Glewitz *D* 10 C4
Gloggnitz *A* 38 B4
Glostrup *DK* 4 B4
Glowe *D* 5 D1
Glöwen *D* 10 A1
Glücksburg *D* 2 C2
Glückstadt *D* 8 C4
Glumso *DK* 4 A3
Gmünd *A* 36 C2
Gmünd *A* 29 F3
Gmund *D* 35 F4
Gmunden *A* 29 D1
Gnarrenburg *D* 8 B3
Gnoien *D* 10 B4
Goch *D* 12 C3
Godelheim *D* 14 B3
Gödre *H* 39 F1
Göhren *D* 5 D1
Goirle *NL* 12 A3
Gokels *D* 2 C1
Golchen *D* 10 C3
Golčův-Jeníkov *CZ* 23 F1
Golczewo *PL* 11 F3
Goldbach *D* 20 B2
Goldberg *D* 10 A3
Goldelund *D* 2 C2
Goldenstedt *D* 8 A2
Goleniów *PL* 11 E3
Gollhofen *D* 20 C1
Golling *A* 36 C4
Golssen *D* 16 C3
Golzow *D* 16 B3
Gommern *D* 15 F3
Gondrecourt *F* 24 A3
Goor *NL* 13 D4
Göpfritz *A* 30 A3
Goppenstein *CH* 33 D2
Göppingen *D* 26 C3
Goričan *HR* 38 C1
Gorinchem *NL* 12 A4
Göritz *D* 11 D2
Gørlev *DK* 3 F4
Görlitz *D* 17 E1
Gornja Radgona *SLO* 38 B2
Gorredijk *NL* 6 C2
Görzke *D* 16 A3
Gorzów Wielkopolski *PL* 11 F1
Górzyca *PL* 17 E4
Gosau *A* 37 D4
Göschenen *CH* 33 F2
Goslar *D* 15 D3
Gossau *CH* 34 B4
Gossensass/Colle Isarco *I* 35 E2

Gössl *A* 37 D4
Gössweinstein *D* 21 E2
Göstling *A* 37 F4
Gotha *D* 21 D4
Göttingen *D* 14 C2
Götzis *A* 34 B3
Gouda *NL* 12 A4
Goumois *CH* 32 C4
Gozdnica *PL* 17 F2
Graal-Müritz *D* 4 B1
Grabow *D* 9 F2
Grächen *CH* 33 D1
Grafenau *D* 28 C3
Gräfenberg *D* 21 E1
Gräfenhainichen *D* 16 B2
Grafenwöhr *D* 21 F1
Grafing *D* 28 A1
Grafrath *D* 27 E2
Gram *DK* 2 C3
Grametten *A* 30 A3
Gramkow *D* 9 F4
Gramzow *D* 11 D2
Granges-sur-Vologne *F* 24 C2
Gransee *D* 10 C2
Grassau *D* 36 B4
Gråsten *DK* 2 C3
Gratkorn *A* 38 A3
Grave *NL* 12 B3
Gravedona *I* 34 B1
Gravellona-Toce *I* 33 E1
Gray *F* 24 A1
Graz *A* 38 A2
Grebenstein *D* 14 B2
Greding *D* 27 F4
Greetsiel *D* 7 E3
Greifenburg *A* 36 C2
Greiffenberg *D* 11 D2
Greifswald *D* 10 C4
Grein *A* 29 F2
Greiz *D* 22 A3
Grenchen *CH* 28 C3
Gressoney-la-Trinité *I* 33 D1
Gresten *A* 29 F1
Greussen *D* 15 E1
Greve Strand *DK* 4 B4
Greven *D* 13 E4
Grevenbroich *D* 12 C2
Grevenbrück *D* 13 E2
Grevenmacher *L* 18 C2
Grevesmühlen *D* 9 E4
Gries in Sellrain *A* 35 E3
Gries-am-Brenner *A* 35 E3
Griesbach *D* 28 C2
Grieskirchen *A* 29 D2
Griffen *A* 37 E2
Grimma *D* 16 B1
Grimmen *D* 10 C4
Grindelwald *CH* 33 E2
Grindsted *DK* 2 C4
Gröbers *D* 16 A2
Gröbming *A* 37 D3
Gröditz *D* 16 C2
Groenlo *NL* 13 D4
Grömitz *D* 9 E4
Gronau *D* 13 D4
Gronau *D* 14 C3
Gröningen *D* 15 E3
Groningen *NL* 7 D3
Grósio *I* 34 C1
Gross Oesingen *D* 9 D1
Gross Räschen *D* 17 D2
Gross Schönebeck *D* 10 C1
Gross-Gerau *D* 19 F2
Gross-Gerungs *A* 29 F2
Gross-Siegharts *A* 30 A3
Gross-Umstadt *D* 20 A2
Grossarl *A* 36 C3
Grossbeeren *D* 16 C4
Grossbreitenbach *D* 21 E3
Grossburgwedel *D* 14 C4
Grossenbrode *D* 3 E1
Grossenhain *D* 16 C1
Grossenkneten *D* 8 A2
Grossenzersdorf *A* 30 C1

Grosshabersdorf *D* 21 D1
Grosshöchstetten *CH* 33 D3
Grosspetersdorf *A* 38 C3
Grossraming *A* 29 E1
Grostenquin *F* 25 D4
Grouw *NL* 6 C3
Grünau *A* 37 D4
Grünberg *D* 20 A4
Grünburg *A* 29 E1
Grundlsee *A* 37 D4
Grünenplan *D* 14 C3
Grünheide *D* 17 D4
Grünstadt *D* 19 E2
Grüsch *CH* 34 B3
Gruyères *CH* 32 C2
Gryfice *PL* 11 F3
Gryfino *PL* 11 E2
Gryfów Śląski *PL* 23 F4
Gschnitz *A* 35 E3
Gschwend *D* 26 C3
Gstaad *CH* 33 D2
Gstadt *D* 28 B1
Gsteig *CH* 33 D2
Guben *D* 17 E3
Gubin *PL* 17 E3
Gudhjem *DK* 5 F3
Gudow *D* 9 E3
Guebwiller *F* 25 D2
Güglingen *D* 26 B4
Guldborg *DK* 4 A2
Gummersbach *D* 13 E1
Gumpoldskirchen *A* 30 C1
Gumtow *D* 10 B2
Gundelfingen *D* 27 D3
Gundelsheim *D* 20 B1
Gunten *CH* 33 D3
Güntersberge *D* 15 E2
Güntersblum *D* 19 F2
Günzburg *D* 27 D2
Gunzenhausen *D* 27 E4
Gurk *A* 37 E2
Gurtnellen *CH* 33 F2
Güssing *A* 38 C2
Güstrow *D* 10 B3
Gutenstein *A* 38 B4
Gütersloh *D* 14 A3
Guttannen *CH* 33 E2
Gützkow *D* 10 C3
Gwatt *CH* 33 D3
Gy *F* 24 A1
Győr *H* 39 E4

H

Haag *A* 29 E1
Haag *D* 28 A2
Haag am Hausruck *A* 29 D2
Haaksbergen *NL* 13 D4
Haar *D* 27 F2
Haaren *D* 14 A2
Haarlem *NL* 6 A1
Habartice *CZ* 23 F4
Habay *B* 18 A2
Hachenburg *D* 19 E4
Hachmühlen *D* 14 C3
Hadamar *D* 19 E3
Haderslev *DK* 2 C3
Hadmersleben *D* 15 E3
Hagen *D* 13 E2
Hagen *D* 8 B3
Hagenow *D* 9 E3
Hagondange *F* 18 B1
Haguenau *F* 25 E3
Hahn *D* 8 A3
Hahnbach *D* 21 F1
Hahót *H* 39 D2
Haigerloch *D* 26 A2
Hainburg *A* 31 D1
Hainfeld *A* 30 B1
Hainichen *D* 22 C4
Halámky *CZ* 29 F3

Halberstadt D	15	E3
Haldensee A	35	D4
Haldensleben D	15	F4
Halk DK	3	D3
Hall in Tirol A	35	E3
Halle D	14	A3
Halle D	16	A2
Hallein A	36	C4
Hallenberg D	14	A1
Hallstatt A	37	D4
Halsskov DK	3	F3
Haltern D	13	D3
Halver D	13	E2
Hambergen D	8	B3
Hamburg D	9	D3
Hamdorf D	2	C1
Hämeler Wald D	15	D4
Hameln D	14	B3
Hamersleben D	15	E3
Hamm D	13	E3
Hammelburg D	20	C3
Hamminkeln D	13	D3
Hamoir B	18	B4
Han-sur-Lesse B	18	A3
Hanau D	20	A3
Handegg CH	33	E2
Hanerau-		
Hademarschen D	2	C1
Hankensbüttel D	9	D1
Hann-Münden D	14	C2
Hannover D	14	C4
Hannuit (Hannut) B	12	A1
Hannut (Hannuit) B	12	A1
Hanstedt D	9	D2
Harburg D	9	D3
Harburg D	27	D3
Hårby DK	3	D3
Hardegg A	30	B3
Hardegsen D	14	C2
Hardenberg NL	7	D1
Harderwijk NL	6	B1
Hardeshøj DK	3	D3
Hardheim D	20	B2
Haren D	7	E2
Haren NL	7	D3
Haren NL	7	D3
Hårlev DK	4	B3
Harlingen NL	6	B3
Harlösa S	5	D4
Harndrup DK	3	D4
Haroué F	24	B3
Harpstedt D	8	B2
Harrachov CZ	23	F3
Harsefeld D	8	C3
Harsewinkel D	13	F3
Harsum D	14	C4
Hartberg A	38	B3
Hartha D	16	B1
Hartmannshain D	20	B3
Harzgerode D	15	E2
Haselund D	2	C2
Haselünne D	7	E1
Haslach A	29	D2
Haslach D	25	E2
Hasle DK	5	E3
Haslev DK	4	B3
Hassel D	8	B2
Hasselfelde D	15	E2
Hasselt B	12	A2
Hasselt NL	6	C2
Hassfurt D	21	D2
Hasslach D	21	E3
Hassleben D	11	D2
Hatĕ CZ	30	B3
Hattem NL	6	C1
Hattingen D	13	D2
Hattstedt D	2	C1
Haugsdorf A	30	B2
Haunersdorf D	28	B2
Hausach D	25	F2
Häusern D	25	E1
Hausham D	35	F4
Haute-Nendaz CH	33	D1
Havelange B	18	A4
Havelberg D	10	A1
Havlíčkův Brod CZ	22	C1
Havlíčkův Brod CZ	23	F1
Havneby DK	2	B3
Havnsø DK	3	F4
Hayange F	18	B2
Hazlov CZ	22	A2
Hechingen D	26	B2
Hechtel B	12	A2
Hedehusene DK	4	B4
Hedensted DK	3	D4
Heek D	13	D4
Heemstede NL	6	A1
Heerde NL	6	C1
Heerenveen NL	6	C1
Heerlen NL	12	B1
Heeze NL	12	B2
Hegyeshalom H	31	D1
Hegyhátsál H	38	C2
Heide D	2	C1
Heidelberg D	19	F1
Heiden D	13	D3
Heidenau D	23	D4
Heidenheim D	27	D3
Heidenreichstein A	30	A3
Heikendorf D	3	D1
Heilbronn D	26	B4
Heiligenberg D	26	B1
Heiligenblut A	36	B3
Heiligenhafen D	3	E1
Heiligenkreuz A	38	B3
Heiligenstadt D	14	C2
Heilsbronn D	27	E4
Heimertingen D	26	C2
Heino NL	6	C1
Heinsberg D	12	C2
Heiterwang A	35	D4
Hejlsminde DK	3	D3
Heldrungen D	15	E1
Hellendoorn NL	7	D1
Helmond NL	12	B3
Helmstedt D	15	E3
Helsa D	14	C2
Hemau D	28	A3
Hemer D	13	E2
Hèming F	25	D3
Hemmoor D	8	C3
Hemslingen D	8	C2
Hengelo NL	13	D4
Hengersberg D	28	C3
Henne Strand DK	2	B4
Henneberg D	21	D3
Hennef D	13	D1
Henstedt-Ulzburg D	9	D3
Heppenheim D	19	F2
Herbertingen D	26	B2
Herbesthal B	12	B1
Herbeumont B	18	A3
Herborn D	19	F4
Herbrechtingen D	27	D3
Herend H	39	E3
Herentals B	12	A2
Herfolge DK	4	B3
Herford D	14	A3
Hergiswil CH	33	E3
Héricourt F	24	C1
Heringsdorf D	11	D3
Herisau CH	34	B4
Herleshausen D	14	C1
Hermagor A	36	C2
Hermannsburg D	9	D1
Heřmanův Městec CZ	23	F2
Hermeskeil D	18	C2
Herne D	13	D2
Heroldsberg D	21	E1
Herrenberg D	26	B3
Herrnburg D	9	E3
Herrnhut D	23	E4
Herrsching D	27	E1
Hersbruck D	21	E1
Herselt B	12	A2
Herstal B	12	B1
Herzberg D	15	D2
Herzberg D	10	C1
Herzberg D	16	C2
Herzfelde D	17	D4
Herzlake D	7	E1
Herzogenaurach D	21	D1
Herzogenburg A	30	B2
Herzsprung D	10	B2
Hesel D	7	E3
Hesnæs DK	4	B2
Hess Oldendorf D	14	B4
Hessisch-Lichtenau D	14	C1
Hettange-Grande F	18	B2
Hettstedt D	15	F2
Heustreu D	20	C3
Hévíz H	39	D2
Hevlin CZ	30	C3
Hieflau A	37	F4
Hilchenbach D	13	F1
Hildburghausen D	21	D3
Hilden D	13	D2
Hilders D	20	C3
Hildesheim D	14	C3
Hillegom NL	6	A1
Hillerød DK	4	B4
Hilpoltstein D	27	E4
Hilterfingen CH	33	D3
Hilvarenbeek NL	12	A3
Hilversum NL	6	B1
Himmelpforten D	8	C3
Hindelang D	35	D4
Hinterrhein CH	34	A2
Hintersee D	11	E3
Hinterstoder A	37	E4
Hinterthal A	36	C3
Hintertux A	35	F3
Hinterweidenthal D	19	E1
Hinterzarten D	25	E2
Hirschaid D	21	D2
Hirschau D	21	F1
Hirschberg D	21	F3
Hirschegg A	34	C3
Hirschhorn D	20	A1
Hirsingue F	25	D1
Hitzacker D	9	E2
Hjerpsted DK	2	B3
Hjerting DK	2	B4
Hjorte DK	3	D3
Hlohovec SK	31	E2
Hluboká nad Vltavou CZ	29	E3
Hluk CZ	31	E3
Höchberg D	20	C2
Hochburg A	28	C1
Hochdonn D	8	C4
Hochdorf CH	33	E3
Höchenschwand D	25	E1
Hochfelden F	25	E3
Hochspeyer D	19	E1
Höchst D	20	A2
Höchstädt D	27	D3
Höchstadt D	21	D2
Hockenheim D	19	F1
Hodde DK	2	B4
Hodenhagen D	8	C1
Hodkovice nad		
Mohelkou CZ	23	F3
Hodonín CZ	31	D3
Hodoš SLO	38	C2
Hodošan HR	38	C1
Hof D	21	F3
Hofgeismar D	14	B2
Hofheim D	21	D2
Hőgyész H	39	F1
Hohenau A	31	D2
Hohenberg A	30	B1
Hohenbrunn D	27	F1
Hohenems A	34	C4
Höhenkirchen D	27	F1
Hohenlimburg D	13	E2
Hohenlinden D	28	A2
Hohenlockstedt D	8	C4
Hohenpeissenberg D	27	E1
Hohenschwangau D	35	D4
Hohentauern A	37	E3
Hohenwestedt D	8	C4
Hohne (Belsen) D	8	C1
Hohwacht D	3	E1
Højer DK	2	B3
Højerup DK	4	B3
Holbæk DK	4	A4
Holdorf D	7	F1
Holeby DK	3	F2
Holešov CZ	31	E4
Holič SK	31	D3
Hollabrunn A	30	B2
Holláð H	39	D2
Hollenstedt D	8	C3
Hollfeld D	21	E2
Hollum NL	6	C3
Höllviksnäs S	4	C3
Holmec SLO	37	F1
Holsted DK	2	C4
Holten NL	6	C1
Holwerd NL	6	C3
Holzdorf D	16	C2
Holzgau A	35	D3
Holzkirchen D	27	F1
Holzminden D	14	C3
Homberg D	20	B4
Homberg D	14	B1
Homburg D	19	D1
Hönebach D	14	C1
Høng DK	3	F4
Hoogeveen NL	7	D2
Hoogezand NL	7	D3
Hoogkarspel NL	6	B2
Hooksiel D	8	A3
Höör S	5	D4
Hoorn NL	6	B2
Hopfgarten A	36	A3
Hopsten D	7	E1
Hoptrup DK	2	C3
Hora-Sv-Šebestiána CZ	22	C3
Horažďovice CZ	29	D4
Horb D	26	A3
Horbelev DK	4	B2
Hörby S	5	D4
Horgen CH	33	F3
Hořice CZ	23	F3
Horitschon A	38	C3
Horn A	30	B2
Horn D	26	A1
Horn D	14	B3
Hornberg D	25	F2
Hornburg D	15	D3
Horne DK	3	D3
Horneburg D	8	C3
Horni Cerekev CZ	30	A4
Horni Lideč CZ	31	F3
Horni Planá CZ	29	D3
Horni Vltavice CZ	29	D3
Hörnum D	2	B2
Hořovice CZ	23	D2
Hørsholm DK	4	B4
Horšovský Týn CZ	22	B1
Horst D	9	E3
Horst NL	12	C3
Hörstel D	13	E4
Horstmar D	13	E4
Hørve DK	4	A4
Horw CH	33	E3
Hospental CH	33	F2
Hostomice CZ	23	D2
Hotton B	18	A4
Houdelaincourt F	24	A3
Houffalize B	18	B3
Hove DK	4	A4
Hövelhof D	14	A3
Höxter D	14	B3
Hoya D	8	B2
Hoyerswerda D	17	D2
Hrádek CZ	30	C3
Hrádek nad Nisou CZ	23	E4
Hranice CZ	31	E4
Hřensko CZ	23	D4
Hrob CZ	23	D3
Hrotovice CZ	30	B3
Hrušovany CZ	30	C3
Huben A	36	B2
Hüfingen D	25	F2

Huizen NL 6 A2
Huizen NL .... 6 BI
Hulín CZ 31 E4
Humble DK 3 E2
Humlebæk DK 4 B4
Humpolec CZ .... 23 FI
Hünfeld D 20 C4
Hungen D 20 A3
Hurbanovo SK 39 F4
Hurva S 5 D4
Husinec CZ 29 D3
Hustopeče CZ 30 C3
Husum D 2 C2
Hüttschlag A 36 C3
Huttwil CH 33 E3
Huy B 18 A4

I

Ibbenburen D 13 E4
Ichenhausen D 27 D2
Idar-Oberstein D 19 D2
Idstein D 19 F3
Igal H .... 39 EI
Igls A 35 E3
Iharosberény H .... 39 DI
IJmuiden NL 6 A2
Ilanz CH 34 B2
Illertissen D 26 C2
Illingen D 26 B4
Illmitz A 39 D4
Ilmenau D 21 D4
Iłowa PL 17 F2
Ilsenburg D 15 D3
Ilshofen D 26 C4
Immenstaad D .... 26 BI
Immenstadt D 34 C4
Imst A 35 D3
Ingelheim D 19 E2
Ingolstadt D 27 F3
Ingwiller F 25 E4
Innertkirchen CH 33 E2
Innichen/San Candido I ... 36 A2
Inning D .... 27 EI
Innsbruck A 35 E3
Ins CH 32 C3
Insko PL 11 F2
Interlaken CH 33 E2
Intra I .... 33 FI
Inzell D 36 B4
Iphofen D 20 C2
Irdning A 37 D3
Iregszemcse H 39 F2
Ischgl A 34 C3
Iselle I .... 33 EI
Iselsberg A 36 B2
Iserlohn D 13 E2
Ismaning D 27 F2
Isny D 34 C4
Isselburg D 12 C3
Istha D 14 B2
Itzehoe D 8 C4
Ivančice CZ 30 C3
Izernore F 32 A2

J

Jablonec nad Nisou CZ 23 F3
Jablonica SK 31 E2
Jablonné v Podještědí CZ ... 23 E3
Jáchymov CZ 22 B3
Jade D 8 A3
Jagel D 2 C2
Jægerspris DK 4 B4
Jagsthausen D .... 20 BI
Jánosháza H 39 D3
Jánossomorja H 39 D4

Janovice nad Úhlavou CZ ... 28 C4
Jarmen D 10 C3
Jarny F .... 18 BI
Jaroměřice
    nad Rokytnou CZ 30 B3
Jasień PL 17 F2
Jaun CH 33 D2
Jävenitz D 15 F4
Jedovnice CZ 31 D4
Jelling DK 2 C4
Jels DK 2 C3
Jemnice CZ 30 B3
Jena D 21 F4
Jenbach A 35 F3
Jeneč CZ 23 D2
Jennersdorf A 38 C2
Jerichow D 16 A4
Jerxheim D 15 E3
Jesberg D .... 14 BI
Jesenice A .... 37 DI
Jesenice CZ 22 C2
Jessen D 16 B2
Jevenstedt D .... 2 CI
Jever D 7 F3
Jevíčko CZ 30 C4
Jevišovice CZ 30 B3
Jezersko SLO .... 37 EI
Jičín CZ 23 F3
Jihlava CZ 30 B4
Jilemnice CZ 23 F3
Jílové u Prahy CZ 23 E2
Jimramov CZ 30 C4
Jince CZ .... 23 DI
Jindřichův Hradec CZ 29 F3
Jirkov CZ 22 C3
Joachimsthal D .... 11 DI
Jodoigne B .... 12 AI
Johanngeorgenstadt D 22 B3
Joinville F 24 A3
Jördenstorf D 10 B3
Jougne F 32 B3
Joure NL 6 C2
Judenburg A 37 E3
Juelsminde DK 3 D4
Juist D 7 E4
Jülich D .... 12 CI
Jussey F 24 B2
Jüterbog D 16 C3
Jyderup DK 3 F4
Jyllinge DK 4 B4

K

Kaarssen D 9 E2
Kaatsheuvel NL 12 A3
Kácov CZ .... 23 EI
Kadaň CZ 22 C3
Kadarkút H .... 39 EI
Kågeröd S 4 C4
Kahla D 21 F4
Kaindorf A 38 B3
Kaisersesch D 19 D3
Kaiserslautern D .... 19 EI
Kaisheim D 27 E3
Kalbe D .... 9 FI
Kalkar D 12 C3
Kallmünz D 28 A4
Kalná nad Hronom SK ...... 31 FI
Kals A 36 B2
Kalsdorf A 38 A2
Kaltenkirchen D 9 D4
Kaltennordheim D 20 C4
Kalundborg DK 3 F4
Kalvehave DK 4 B2
Kalwang A 37 E3
Kám H 39 D2
Kámen CZ 29 F4
Kamen D 13 E3
Kamenice nad Lipou CZ ... 29 F4
Kamenz D .... 17 DI
Kamień Pomorski PL 11 E3

Kamnik SLO .... 37 EI
Kamp Lintfort D 12 C3
Kampen D 2 B3
Kampen NL 6 C2
Kandel D 25 F4
Kandern D .... 25 EI
Kandersteg CH 33 D2
Kapfenberg A 38 A3
Kaplice CZ 29 E3
Kaposvár H .... 39 EI
Kappeln D 3 D2
Kaprun A 36 B3
Kapuvar H 39 D4
Kardašova-Řečice CZ 29 F4
Karise DK 4 B3
Karlovy Vary CZ 22 B2
Karlshafen D 14 C2
Karlsruhe D 25 F4
Karlstadt D 20 C2
Karlštejn CZ 23 D2
Karlstift A 29 F2
Karlsund Strand DK 4 B4
Karow D 10 B3
Karrebæksminde DK 4 A3
Karstadt D 10 A2
Kasejovice CZ 29 D4
Kašperské Hory CZ 29 D4
Kassel D 14 B2
Kastellaun D 19 D3
Kasterlee B 12 A2
Kastl D 27 F4
Kastorf D 9 E3
Kastrup DK 4 C4
Katerbow D 10 B2
Katlenburg-Duhm D 14 C2
Katovice CZ 29 D4
Kaub D 19 E3
Kaufbeuren D .... 27 DI
Kaufering D 27 E2
Kaufungen D 14 C2
Kauns A 35 D3
Kävlinge S 4 C4
Kaysersberg F 25 D2
Kaznějov CZ 22 C2
Kdyně CZ 28 C4
Kefermarkt A 29 E2
Kehl D 25 E3
Kelberg D 19 D3
Kelbra D 15 E2
Kelheim D 28 A3
Kellenhusen D .... 3 EI
Kellinghusen D 8 C4
Kemberg D 16 B2
Kemenný Újezd CZ 29 E3
Kemnath D 21 F2
Kemnitz D 11 D4
Kempen D 12 C2
Kempten D .... 27 DI
Kenzingen D 25 E2
Kerken D 12 C2
Kerkrade NL .... 12 BI
Kerpen D .... 12 CI
Kerteminde DK 3 E4
Kerzers CH 33 D3
Keszthely H 39 D2
Kettwig D 13 D2
Ketzin D 16 B4
Keula D 15 D2
Kevelaer D 12 C3
Kiefersfelden D 36 A4
Kiel D .... 3 DI
Kiental CH 33 D2
Kindberg A 38 A3
Kindelbrück D .... 15 EI
Kirchbach A 38 B2
Kirchberg A 36 B3
Kirchberg D 19 D3
Kirchberg an 26 C4
Kirchberg an
    der Pielach A .... 30 AI
Kirchdorf an
    der Krems A .... 29 EI
Kirchenlamitz D 21 F2
Kirchenthumbach D 21 F2

Kirchhain D 20 B4
Kirchheim D 20 B4
Kirchheim unter Teck D ... 26 B3
Kirchheimbolanden D 19 E2
Kirchlinteln D 8 C2
Kirchschlag A 38 C3
Kirchundem D .... 13 FI
Kirke Hvalso DK 4 A4
Kirn D 19 D2
Kirtorf D 20 B4
Kisbér H 39 F3
Kisslegg D .... 26 CI
Kittsee A .... 31 DI
Kitzbühel A 36 B3
Kitzingen D 20 C2
Kladno CZ 23 D2
Klagenfurt A 37 E2
Klanxbüll D 2 B3
Klášterec nad Ohří CZ 22 C3
Klatovy CZ 28 C4
Klaus an der
    Pyhrnbahn A 37 E4
Klausdorf D 16 C3
Klausen/Chiusa I 35 E2
Klazienaveen NL 7 D2
Kleinhaugsdorf A 30 B3
Klemensker DK 5 E3
Klenčí CZ 28 C4
Kleve D 12 C3
Kliczków PL .... 17 FI
Klietz D .... 10 AI
Klingenbach A 38 C4
Klingenthal D 22 B3
Klink D 10 B3
Klixbüll D 2 B2
Kłodawa PL .... 11 FI
Klösterle A 34 C3
Klosterneuburg A 30 C2
Klosters CH 34 C2
Klötze D .... 9 EI
Klütz D 9 E4
Kniebis D 25 F3
Knittelfeld A 37 F3
Knudshoved DK 3 E3
Kobarid SLO .... 36 CI
København DK 4 B4
Koblenz D 19 E3
Kochel D 35 E4
Köflach A 37 F2
Køge DK 4 B3
Kojetin CZ 31 D4
Kolárovo SK 39 F4
Kołbaskowo PL 11 E2
Kolbermoor D .... 28 AI
Kolby Kås DK 3 E4
Kołczewo PL 11 E3
Kolding DK 2 C4
Kolin CZ 23 F2
Kölleda D .... 15 EI
Kollund DK 2 C2
Koloveč CZ .... 22 BI
Komárno SK 39 F4
Komárom H 39 F4
Komló H .... 39 FI
Køng DK 4 A3
Konice CZ 31 D4
Königs-Wusterhausen D ... 17 D3
Königsbrück D .... 17 DI
Königsbrunn D 27 E2
Königsee D 21 E4
Königsfeld D 25 F2
Königshofen D .... 20 BI
Königslutter D 15 E4
Königssee D 36 C4
Königstein D 19 F3
Königstein D 23 D4
Königswiesen A 29 F2
Königswinter D 19 D4
Köniz CH 33 D3
Könnern D 15 F2
Konopiště CZ .... 23 EI
Konstanz CZ .... 26 BI
Konz D 18 C2

KÖLN

NEUSS — DÜSSELDORF — WUPPERTAL

Rheindorf — Opladen

Sinnersdorf — Schlebusch — LEVERKUSEN — Odenthal

Heimersdorf — Flittard

Pulheim — Höhenhaus — Bergisch Gladbach

Ossendorf — Mülheim

Nippes — Bensberg

Ehrenfeld — Deutz — Königsforst

AACHEN — Lindenthal — Rath

Frechen — Zollstock

Porz

Hürth — Rondorf — Rodenkirchen

FRANKFURT

Meschenich — Zündorf Wahn — Köln/Bonn

Brühl — BONN

0   5 km

Köpernitz D 10 C2
Kópháza H 38 C4
Kopidlno CZ 23 F3
Kopperby D 3 D2
Koprivnica HR .... 39 DI
Korbach D 14 B2
Korczyców PL 17 E3
Korinth DK 3 E3
Körmend H 38 C2
Korneuburg A 30 C2
Kornwestheim D 26 B3
Korpavár H .... 39 DI
Korsør DK 3 F3
Korup DK 3 E4
Koryčany CZ 31 D3
Koserow D 11 D4
Košetice CZ .... 23 FI
Kössen A 36 B4
Kostelec nad
   Černými CZ 23 E2
Kostelec nad Labem CZ ... 23 E2
Kostrzyn PL 17 E4
Köszeg H 38 C3
Köthen D 16 A2
Kötschach-Mauthen A ... 36 C2
Kotten NL 13 D3
Kötzting D 28 C4
Kozolupy CZ .... 22 CI
Kożuchów PL 17 F2
Kragenæs DK 3 F2
Krajnik Dolny PL 11 E2
Krakow am See D 10 B3
Kralovice CZ 22 C2
Kralupy nad Vltavou CZ ... 23 D2
Kranenburg D 12 C3
Kranichfeld D 21 E4
Kranj SLO .... 37 EI
Kranjska Gora SLO .... 37 DI
Krapina HR .... 38 BI
Kraslice CZ 22 B3
Krásná Lípa CZ 23 E4
Krauchenwies D 26 B2
Krefeld D 12 C2
Kremmen D .... 10 CI

Krems A 30 B2
Kremsmünster A .... 29 EI
Kreuth D 35 F4
Kreuzlingen CH .... 26 BI
Kreuztal D .... 13 EI
Krieglach A 38 B3
Krimml A 36 A3
Krimpen aan
   den IJssel NL 12 A4
Kristinehov S 5 D4
Křivoklát CZ 23 D2
Křižanov CZ 30 B4
Krogsbølle DK 3 E4
Kroměříž CZ 31 E4
Kronach D 21 E3
Kröpelin D 10 A4
Kropp D .... 2 CI
Kroppenstedt D 15 E3
Kropstädt D 16 B3
Krosno Odrzanskie PL ... 17 F3
Krumbach D 27 D2
Krumpendorf A 37 E2
Krün D 35 E4
Krupá CZ 22 C2
Kruså DK 2 C2
Krzęcin PL 11 F2
Krzeszyce PL 17 F4
Kúblis CH 34 C3
Kuchl A 36 C4
Kufstein A 36 A4
Kühlungsborn D 10 A4
Kuhstedt D 8 B3
Kühtai A 35 E3
Kulhuse DK 4 B4
Kulmbach D 21 E2
Kunovice CZ 31 E3
Kunrau D 15 E4
Kunštát CZ 30 C4
Kunžak CZ 30 A3
Künzelsau D 26 C4
Kupferberg D 21 E2
Kupferzell D 26 C2
Kurd H .... 39 FI
Kuřim CZ 30 C4

Kusel D 19 D2
Küssnacht CH 33 F3
Kutná Hora CZ 23 F2
Kúty SK 31 D2
Kværndrup DK 3 E3
Kyjov CZ 31 D3
Kyllburg D 18 C3
Kyritz D .... 10 BI
Kyšice CZ 23 D2

L

L'Isle-sur-le-Doubs F .... 24 CI
La Bresse F 24 C2
La Chaux-de-Fonds CH ... 32 C3
La Clusaz F .... 32 BI
La Cluse F 32 A2
La Cluse-et-Mijoux F 32 B3
La Cure F 32 B2
La Neuveville CH 32 C3
La Petite-Pierre F 25 D4
La Punt CH 34 C2
La Roche-en-Ardenne B ... 18 A3
La Roche-sur-Foron F ... 32 BI
La Thuile I .... 32 CI
La Wantzenau F 25 E3
Laa an der Thaya A 30 C2
Laage D 10 B4
Laarbruch D 12 C3
Laasphe D .... 13 FI
Låbod H .... 39 EI
Laboe D .... 3 DI
Ladbergen D 13 E4
Ladby DK 3 E3
Laferté F 24 A2
Lage D 14 B3
Łagów PL 17 F3
Lahnstein D 19 E3
Lahr D 25 E2
Laichingen D 26 C2
Laimbach A 29 F2

Lakolk DK 2 B3
Lam D 28 C4
Lamarche F 24 B2
Lambach A .... 29 DI
Lambrecht D .... 19 FI
Lamprechtshausen A .... 28 CI
Lamsfeld D 17 D3
Lamstedt D 8 B3
Lana I 35 E2
Landau D .... 19 EI
Landau D 28 B3
Landeck A 35 D3
Landesbergen D .... 8 BI
Landkirchen D .... 3 FI
Landquart CH 34 B3
Landsberg D .... 27 EI
Landsberg D 16 A2
Landshut D 28 A2
Landskrona S 4 C4
Landstuhl D .... 19 DI
Langballig D 3 D2
Langelsheim D 15 D3
Langen A 34 C3
Langen D 20 A2
Langen D 8 B3
Langenargen D 34 B4
Langenburg D 26 C4
Längenfeld A 35 E3
Langenfeld D 13 D2
Langenhahn D 19 E4
Langenisarhofen D 28 C3
Langenlois A 30 B2
Langennaundorf D 16 C2
Langenselbold D 20 B3
Langenthal CH 33 E3
Langenwang A 38 B3
Langenzenn D .... 21 DI
Langeoog D 7 E4
Langeskov DK 3 E3
Langewiese D 14 A2
Langnau im
   Emmental CH 33 E3
Langø DK 3 E2
Langquaid D 28 A3
Langres F 24 A2
Langula D .... 15 DI
Langwarden D 8 A3
Langwedel D 8 B2
Langweid D 27 E2
Lanžhot CZ 31 D3
Lapoutroie F 25 D2
Larochette L 18 B2
Laško SLO .... 38 AI
Lassan D 11 D3
Lastrup D 7 F2
Lathen D 7 E2
Laucha D .... 15 FI
Lauchhammer D 17 D2
Lauenau D 14 C4
Lauenburg D 9 D3
Lauenstein D 23 D4
Lauf D .... 21 EI
Laufen CH 33 D4
Laufen D .... 28 CI
Laufenburg CH 33 E4
Laufenburg D .... 25 EI
Lauffen D 26 B4
Lauingen D 27 D3
Laupen CH 33 D3
Laupheim D 26 C2
Lausanne CH 32 C2
Lauterbach D 20 B4
Lauterbourg F 25 F4
Lauterbrunnen CH 33 E2
Lauterecken D 19 D2
Lauterhofen D 27 F4
Lauwersoog NL 7 D3
Lavamünd A 37 F2
Lavelsloh D 14 B4
Lavis I .... 35 EI
Làzne Kynžvart CZ 22 B2
Le Bourget F .... 32 AI
Le Châtelard F .... 32 AI
Le Hohwald F 25 D3

Le Locle CH	32	C3
Le Markstein F	25	D2
Le Russey F	32	C4
Le Thillot F	24	C2
Lebach D	18	C2
Leberec CZ	23	F3
Lebus D	17	E4
Lech A	34	C3
Lechovice CZ	30	C3
Leck D	2	C2
Łęczyca PL	11	F2
Ledeč nad Sázavou CZ	23	F1
Leek NL	7	D3
Leer D	7	E3
Leerdam NL	12	A4
Leese D	8	B1
Leeuwarden NL	6	C3
Legden D	13	D4
Lehnice SK	31	E1
Lehnin D	16	B3
Lehrberg D	21	D1
Lehre D	15	D4
Lehrte D	14	C4
Leibnitz A	38	B2
Leiden NL	6	A1
Leinefelde D	15	D2
Leipheim D	27	D2
Leipzig D	16	B1
Leisnig D	16	B1
Leissigen CH	33	D2
Leitzkau D	16	A3
Leknica PL	17	E2
Lelystad NL	6	B1
Lembach F	25	E4
Lemförde D	8	A1
Lemgo D	14	B3
Lemke D	8	B1
Lemmer NL	6	C2
Lenart SLO	38	B1
Lend A	36	C3
Lendava SLO	38	C1
Lengerich D	13	F4
Lenggries D	35	F4
Lengyeltóti H	39	E2
Lenk CH	33	D2
Lenna I	34	B1
Lenno I	34	A1
Lenora CZ	29	D3
Lensahn D	3	E1
Lentföhrden D	9	D4
Lenti H	38	C1
Lenting D	27	F3
Lenzburg CH	33	E4
Lenzen D	9	F2
Lenzerheide CH	34	B2
Lenzkirch D	25	F1
Leoben A	37	F3
Leogang A	36	B3
Leonberg D	26	B3
Leopoldsburg B	12	A2
Leopoldsdorf A	30	C1
Lepoglava HR	38	B1
Lepsény H	39	F2
Lermoos A	35	D3
Les Contamines-Montjoie F	32	B1
Les Diablerets CH	32	C2
Les Gets F	32	B2
Les Haudères CH	33	C1
Les Houches F	32	C1
Les Planches-en-Montagne F	32	B3
Les Rousses F	32	B2
Les Trois-Epis F	25	D2
Lésna PL	23	F4
Lésniów Wielki PL	17	F3
Lesum D	8	B2
Letenye H	38	C1
Letmathe D	13	F4
Letovice CZ	30	C4
Letschin D	17	E4
Leuk CH	33	D2
Leukerbad CH	33	D2
Leuna D	16	A1
Leutasch A	35	E3
Leutenberg D	21	E3
Leutkirch D	26	C1
Leutschach A	38	A2
Leverkusen D	13	D1
Levier F	32	B3
Leysin CH	32	C2
Libáň CZ	23	F3
Libochovice CZ	23	D3
Libramont B	18	A3
Lich D	20	A3
Lichtenau D	14	B2
Lichtenberg D	21	F3
Lichtenfels D	21	E2
Lichtenstein D	22	B4
Lichtenvoorde NL	13	D4
Liebenau D	8	B1
Liebenwalde D	10	C1
Lieberose D	17	E3
Liège (Luik) B	12	B1
Lienz A	36	B2
Liestal CH	33	E4
Liezen A	37	E4
Ligneuville B	18	B4
Ligny-en-Barrois F	24	A4
Lilienfeld A	30	B1
Lille DK	4	B4
Lillerød DK	4	B4
Limburg D	19	E3
Limhamn S	4	C4
Lindau D	34	C4
Lindau D	16	A3
Lindenberg D	34	C4
Lindenfels D	20	A2
Linderhof D	35	E4
Lindern D	7	F2
Lindow D	10	C1
Lingen D	7	E1
Linthal CH	34	A3
Lintzel D	9	D2
Linz A	29	E2
Linz D	19	D4
Lipiany PL	11	F1
Lipinki Łużyckie PL	17	E2
Lipnik nad Bečvou CZ	31	E4
Lipno CZ	29	E2
Lippstadt D	13	F3
Liselund DK	4	B2
Lišov CZ	29	E3
Lisse NL	6	A1
List D	2	B3
Litoměřice CZ	23	D3
Litvinov CZ	22	C3
Livigno I	34	C2
Ljubelj SLO	37	E1
Ljubno SLO	37	F1
Ljutomer SLO	38	C1
Lnáře CZ	29	D4
Löbau D	17	E1
Lobenstein D	21	F3
Löbnitz D	4	B1
Loburg D	16	A3
Locarno CH	33	F1
Loccum D	14	B4
Lochem NL	12	C4
Lockenhaus A	38	C3
Löcknitz D	11	E2
Löderup S	5	E3
Lofer A	36	B4
Loga D	7	E3
Løgumkloster DK	2	C3
Lohals DK	3	E3
Lohberg D	28	C4
Lohne D	8	A1
Löhne D	14	B4
Lohnsfeld D	19	E2
Lohr D	20	B2
Loitz D	10	C4
Løjt Kirkeby DK	2	C3
Lomma S	4	C4
Lomnice nad Lužnici CZ	29	F1
Longeau F	24	A2
Longuyon F	18	A2
Longwy F	18	B2
Löningen D	7	F2
Lons-le-Saunier F	32	A3
Loosdorf A	30	A1
Lorcé B	18	B4
Lorch D	19	E3
Lorch D	26	C3
Lorentzen F	25	D4
Lörrach D	25	E1
Lorup D	7	E2
Losenstein A	29	E1
Losheim D	18	C4
Losheim D	18	C2
Lossburg D	25	F3
Lotte D	13	F4
Louny CZ	23	D3
Lovasberény H	39	F3
Lövö H	39	D3
Lovosice CZ	23	D3
Löwenberg D	10	C1
Lozzo di Cadore I	36	B1
Lubań PL	17	F1
Lübbecke D	14	A4
Lübben D	17	D3
Lübbenau D	17	D2
Lübbow D	9	E2
Lübeck D	9	E4
Lubenec CZ	22	C2
Lubniewice PL	17	F4
Lubsko PL	17	E2
Lübtheen D	9	E2
Lübz D	10	A3
Lüchow D	9	E2
Luckau D	17	D2
Luckenwalde D	16	C3
Lückstedt D	9	F1
Ludbreg HR	38	C1
Lüdenscheid D	13	E2
Lüderitz D	15	F4
Lüdinghausen D	13	E3
Ludwigsburg D	26	B3
Ludwigshafen D	19	F1
Ludwigshafen D	26	B1
Ludwigslust D	9	F2
Ludwigsstadt D	21	E3
Lugano CH	34	A1
Lügde D	14	B3
Luik (Liège) B	12	B1
Luino I	33	F1
Lukovica SLO	37	E1
Lummen B	12	A2
Lund S	4	C4
Lundeborg DK	3	E3
Lunden D	2	C1
Lüneburg D	9	D2
Lünen D	13	E3
Lunéville F	24	C3
Lungern CH	33	E3
Lünne D	7	E1
Lunz A	37	F4
Lure F	24	C1
Lustenau A	34	C4
Lutherstadt Eisleben D	15	F2
Lutherstadt Wittenberg D	16	B3
Lütjenburg D	3	E1
Lützen D	16	A1
Lutzmannsburg A	38	C3
Lützow D	9	E3
Luxembourg L	18	B2
Luxeuil-les-Bains F	24	C2
Luzern CH	33	E3
Lwówek Śląski PL	23	F4
Lychen D	10	C2
Lysá nad Labem CZ	23	E2
Lyss CH	33	D3

M

Maaseik B	12	B2
Maasmechelen B	12	B2
Maastricht NL	12	B1
Mackenrode D	15	D2
Macugnaga I	33	E1
Made NL	12	A3
Madésimo I	34	B2
Madonna di Campiglio I	35	D1
Magdeburg D	15	F3
Maglehem S	5	E4
Maglehøj Strand DK	3	F2
Maïche F	32	C4
Maienfeld CH	34	B3
Mainburg D	27	F3
Mainz D	19	F3
Maisach D	27	E2
Maissau A	30	B2
Makov SK	31	F4
Malacky SK	31	D2
Malbuisson F	32	B3
Malchin D	10	B3
Malchow D	10	B3
Malé I	35	D1
Malente-Gremsmühlen D	3	E1
Mallersdorf D	28	B3
Málles Venosta/Mals im Vinschgau I	35	D2
Mallnitz A	36	C2
Malmédy B	18	B4
Malmö S	4	C4
Maloja CH	34	B2
Mals im Vinschgau/Málles Venosta I	35	D2
Malšice CZ	29	E4
Manching D	27	F3
Manderscheid D	18	C3
Manétin CZ	22	C2
Mánfa H	39	F1
Maniago I	36	B1
Mank A	30	A1
Mannheim D	19	F1
Manschnow D	17	E4
Mansfeld D	15	E2
Marbach D	26	B4
Marburg D	20	A4
Marcali H	39	E1
Marchaux F	32	B4
Marche-en-Famenne B	18	A3
Marchegg A	31	D2
Marckolsheim F	25	E2
Maria Laach D	19	D3
Maria Taferl A	30	A2
Maria Wörth A	37	D2
Mariánské Lázně CZ	22	B2
Mariazell A	38	A4
Maribo DK	3	F2
Maribor SLO	38	B1
Marieholm S	4	C4
Marielyst DK	4	A2
Marienberg D	22	C3
Marienborn D	15	E3
Markdorf D	26	B1
Märkisch Buchholz D	17	D3
Markleugast D	21	F2
Markneukirchen D	22	A3
Markranstädt D	16	A1
Markt Bibart D	21	D1
Markt Erlbach D	21	D1
Markt St Florian A	29	E1
Markt St Martin A	38	C3
Markt-Indersdorf D	27	E2
Marktbreit D	20	C2
Marktheidenfeld D	20	B2
Marktl D	28	B2
Marktoberdorf D	27	D1
Marktredwitz D	22	A2
Marktzeuln D	21	E2
Marl D	13	D3
Marlenheim F	25	E3
Marlow D	10	B4
Marmoutier F	25	D3
Marnay F	32	A4
Marne D	8	B4
Marnitz D	10	A2

Marnitz D 10 A2
Marquartstein D 36 B4
Marsberg D 14 B2
Marstal DK 3 E2
Martelange B 18 B3
Martigny CH 32 C1
Martina/Martinsbruck CH ... 35 D2
Martinsbruck/Martina CH ... 35 D2
Martofte DK 3 E4
Marxwalde D 17 D4
Marxzell D 26 A3
Marzahna D 16 B3
Marzahne D 16 B4
Maschen D 9 D3
Masevaux F 25 D1
Maszecwo PL 17 E3
Maszewo PL 11 F2
Mathay F 32 C4
Matrei am Brenner A 35 E3
Matrei in Osttirol A 36 B2
Mattersburg A 38 C4
Mattighofen A 28 C1
Mattsee A 28 C1
Mauerkirchen A 28 C2
Maulbronn D 26 A4
Mautern A 37 F3
Mauterndorf A 37 D3
Mauth D 29 D3
Mauthausen A 29 E2
Mauvoisin CH 33 D1
Mayen D 19 D3
Mayrhofen A 35 F3
Mechernich D 18 C4
Meckenbeuren D 26 B1
Medebach D 14 A2
Medemblik NL 6 B2
Medved'ov SK 39 E4
Medvode SLO 37 E1
Meerane D 22 B4
Meersburg D 26 B1
Megève F 32 B1
Meijel NL 12 B2
Meilen CH 33 F3
Meine D 15 D4
Meinerzhagen D 13 E2
Meiningen D 21 D3
Meiringen CH 33 E2
Meisenheim D 19 E2
Meissen D 16 C1
Meitingen D 27 E2
Mel I 36 A1
Melbeck D 9 D2
Meldorf D 2 C1
Mélisey F 24 C2
Melk A 30 A2
Melle D 14 A4
Mellendorf D 8 C1
Mellin D 9 E1
Mellrichstadt D 21 D3
Mělník CZ 23 E3
Melsungen D 14 C1
Memmingen D 26 C1
Menággio I 34 A1
Menden D 13 E2
Ménfőcsanak H 39 E4
Mengen D 26 B2
Mengeš SLO 37 E1
Menthon F 32 B1
Meppel NL 6 C2
Meppen D 7 E2
Meran/Merano I 35 E2
Merano/Meran I 35 E2
Měřín CZ 30 B4
Mering D 27 E2
Merkendorf D 27 E4
Merklingen D 26 C2
Merligen CH 33 D2
Mern DK 4 B3
Mernye H 39 E1
Mersch D 12 C1
Mersch L 18 B2
Merseburg D 16 A2
Merzig D 18 C2
Meschede D 13 F2

Mesinge DK 3 E4
Mesocco CH 34 B2
Mespelbrunn D 20 B2
Messdorf D 9 F1
Messkirch D 26 B2
Messtetten D 26 B2
Mestlin D 10 A3
Metabief F 32 B3
Metnitz A 37 E2
Metten D 28 C3
Mettingen D 13 E4
Mettlach D 18 C2
Mettmann D 13 D2
Metz F 18 B1
Metzervisse F 18 B1
Metzingen D 26 B3
Meuselwitz D 16 A1
Meyenburg D 10 B2
Mezőörs H 39 E3
Mezőszilas H 39 F2
Mezzolombardo I 35 E1
Micheldorf A 37 E4
Michelstadt D 20 A2
Middelfart DK 3 D4
Midlum D 8 B4
Midsland NL 6 B3
Mieders A 35 E3
Międzdroje PL 11 E3
Międzyrzecz PL 17 F4
Miedzywodzie PL 11 E4
Miesbach D 35 F4
Mieste D 15 E4
Miesterhorst D 15 E4
Mieszkowice PL 11 E1
Mihla D 15 D1
Mijoux F 32 A2
Mikulov CZ 30 C3
Milevsko CZ 29 E4
Milín CZ 23 D1
Millstatt A 37 D2
Milmersdorf D 11 D2
Milow D 9 F2
Miltach D 28 C4
Miltenberg D 20 B2

Mimoň CZ 23 E3
Mindelheim D 27 D2
Minden D 14 B4
Minsen D 8 A4
Mirebeau F 24 A1
Mirecourt F 24 B3
Mirošov CZ 22 C1
Mirovice CZ 23 D1
Mirow D 10 B2
Mirsk PL 23 F4
Mistelbach A 30 C2
Misurina I 36 A2
Mittelberg A 34 C3
Mittelberg A 35 D3
Mittelberg D 35 D4
Mittenwald D 35 E4
Mittenwalde D 16 C3
Mittenwalde D 11 D2
Mittersill A 36 B3
Mitterteich D 22 A2
Mittweida D 22 B4
Mitwitz D 21 E3
Mladá Boleslav CZ 23 E3
Mladá Vožice CZ 23 E1
Mnich CZ 29 F4
Mnichovo Hradiště CZ 23 E3
Mníšek pod Brdy CZ 23 D2
Moča SK 39 F4
Möckern D 16 A3
Möckmühl D 20 B1
Modave B 18 A4
Mödling A 30 C1
Modra SK 31 D2
Moena I 35 F1
Moers D 12 C2
Moirans-en-Montagne F 32 A2
Mol B 12 A2
Möllbrücke A 36 C2
Möllenbeck D 10 C2
Mölln D 9 E3
Molsheim D 25 E3
Molveno I 35 D1
Mommark DK 3 D4
Mönchdorf A 29 F2

Mönchengladbach D 12 C2
Mönchhof A 31 D1
Mondorf-les-Bains L 18 B2
Mondsee A 28 C1
Monguelfo/Welsberg I 36 A2
Monheim D 27 E3
Monschau D 18 C4
Monsheim D 19 E2
Mont-sous-Vaudrey F 32 A3
Montabaur D 19 E3
Montana CH 33 D2
Montbéliard F 24 C1
Montbenoît F 32 B3
Monthey CH 32 C2
Monthureaux-sur-
        Saône F 24 B2
Montigny-le-Roi F 24 A2
Montmédy F 18 A2
Montmirey F 32 A4
Montreux CH 32 C2
Moordorf D 7 E3
Moosburg D 28 A2
Moosinning D 27 F2
Mór H 39 F3
Moravské Budějovice CZ ... 30 B3
Moravské Lieskové SK 31 E3
Moravský Krumlov CZ 30 C3
Morbach D 19 D2
Morbegno I 34 B1
Mörbisch A 38 C4
Morcote CH 34 A1
Morez F 32 B2
Mörfelden D 19 F2
Morges CH 32 B3
Morgex I 32 C1
Morgins CH 32 C2
Morhange F 24 C4
Moritzburg D 17 D1
Mørkøv DK 4 A4
Morteau F 32 C3
Moryń PL 11 E1
Morzine F 32 C2

Morzycyn PL 11 F2
Mosbach D 20 A1
Moschendorf A 38 C2
Mosonmagyaróvár H 39 D4
Mössingen D 26 B2
Most CZ 22 C3
Mouchard F 32 A3
Moudon CH 32 C3
Mouthe F 32 B3
Mouthier F 32 B3
Moutier CH 33 D4
Mrzeżyno PL 11 F4
Mšeno CZ 23 E3
Much D 13 D1
Mücheln D 15 F1
Mudau D 20 B1
Müden D 9 D2
Mügeln D 16 C1
Muggendorf D 21 E2
Mühlacker D 26 B4
Mühlbach A 36 C3
Mühlberg D 16 C2
Mühldorf D 28 B2
Mühlhausen D 26 C3
Mühlhausen D 15 D1
Mülheim D 19 D3
Mülheim D 13 D2
Mulhouse F 25 D1
Müllheim D 25 E1
Müllrose D 17 E3
Münchberg D 21 F2
Müncheberg D 17 D4
München D 27 F2
Münchhausen D 14 A1
Münchhausen D 16 C2
Munkebo DK 3 E4
Münnerstadt D 20 C3
Münsingen CH 33 D3
Münsingen D 26 B2
Münster CH 33 E2
Münster D 13 E3
Münster D 9 D2
Munster F 25 D2
Münstertal D 25 E1
Münzkirchen A 29 D2
Murau A 37 E3
Murchin D 11 D3
Mureck A 38 B2
Muri CH 33 F4
Murnau D 35 E4
Mürren CH 33 E2
Murrhardt D 26 C4
Murska Sobota SLO 38 C2
Mursko Središće HR 38 C1
Murten CH 32 C3
Mürzsteg A 38 A4
Mürzzuschlag A 38 B4
Musselkanaal NL 7 E2
Müstair CH 35 D2
Muster/Disentis CH 34 A2
Mutterstadt D 19 F1
Myjava SK 31 E3
Myślibórz PL 11 E1
Mýto CZ 22 C1

N

Naarden NL 6 B1
Nabburg D 22 A1
Nadrin B 18 B3
Näfels CH 34 A3
Nagold D 26 A3
Nagyatád H 39 D1
Nagybajom H 39 E1
Nagycenk H 38 C3
Nagygyimót H 39 E3
Nagyigmánd H 39 F4
Nagykanizsa H 39 D1
Nagykónyi H 39 F1
Nagyvázsony H 39 E2
Nahe D 9 D3

Naila D 21 F3
Nakskov DK 3 F2
Náměšt nad Oslavou CZ .. 30 C4
Nancy F 24 C4
Nantua F 32 A2
Nassau D 19 E3
Nassereith A 35 D3
Næstved DK 4 A3
Naturno/Naturns I 35 D2
Naturns/Naturno I 35 D2
Nauders A 35 D2
Nauen D 16 B4
Naumburg D 15 F1
Naunhof D 16 B1
Nebra D 15 F1
Neckarelz D 20 A1
Neckargemünd D 20 A1
Neckargerach D 20 A1
Neckarsteinach D 20 A1
Neckarsulm D 26 B4
Nedelišće HR 38 C1
Neede NL 13 D4
Neermoor D 7 E3
Neheim-Hüsten D 13 E2
Nejdek CZ 22 B3
Nekso DK 5 F2
Nemšová SK 31 F3
Nendeln FL 34 B3
Nepomuk CZ 22 C1
Neratovice CZ 23 E2
Neresheim D 27 D3
Nersingen D 26 C2
Nes NL 6 C3
Nesselwang D 35 D4
Netolice CZ 29 E3
Nettancourt F 24 A4
Nettetal D 12 C2
Neu Darchau D 9 E2
Neu Mukran D 5 D1
Neu-Isenburg D 20 A3
Neu-Moresnet B 12 B1
Neubeckum D 13 F3
Neubrandenburg D 10 C3
Neubukow D 10 A4
Neuburg D 27 E3
Neuchâtel CH 32 C3
Neudorf D 26 A4
Neudorf-Platendorf D .. 15 D4
Neuenburg D 25 D1
Neuenbürg D 26 A3
Neuenburg D 7 F3
Neuenhaus D 7 D1
Neuenkirchen D 8 C2
Neuenwalde D 8 B3
Neuf-Brisach F 25 D2
Neufahrn D 28 B3
Neufchâteau B 18 A3
Neufchâteau F 24 B3
Neufelden A 29 D2
Neugersdorf D 23 E4
Neuhaus D 8 B4
Neuhaus D 14 C3
Neuhaus D 21 E3
Neuhaus D 9 E2
Neuhaus D 21 E1
Neuhaus D 28 C2
Neuhausen am
Rheinfall CH 25 F1
Neuhof D 16 C3
Neuhofen an
der Krems A 29 E1
Neuilly-l'Évêque F 24 A2
Neukalen D 10 C3
Neukirch D 23 D4
Neukirchen A 36 A3
Neukirchen D 2 B3
Neukloster D 10 A3
Neulengbach A 30 B1
Neumarkt A 28 C1
Neumarkt A 37 E2
Neumarkt D 27 F4
Neumarkt-St Veit D 28 B2
Neumorschen D 14 C1
Neumünster D 9 D4

Neunagelberg A 29 F3
Neunburg D 28 B4
Neunkirchen A 38 B4
Neunkirchen D 19 D1
Neuötting D 28 B2
Neupölla A 30 A2
Neuruppin D 10 B1
Neusiedl am See A 31 D1
Neuss D 13 D2
Neustadt D 25 F2
Neustadt D 20 B4
Neustadt D 21 E3
Neustadt D 9 E4
Neustadt D 27 F3
Neustadt D 21 F4
Neustadt D 10 B1
Neustadt D 23 D4
Neustadt am
Rübenberge D 8 C1
Neustadt an der Aisch D .. 21 D1
Neustadt an
der Waldnaab D 22 A1
Neustadt an
der Weinstrasse D 19 E1
Neustadt-Glewe D 9 F2
Neustift A 35 E3
Neustrelitz D 10 C2
Neuves-Maisons F 24 B3
Neuwied D 19 D4
Nickelsdorf A 31 D1
Nidderau D 20 A3
Niebüll D 2 B2
Nieby D 3 D2
Niechorze PL 11 F4
Nieder Stotzingen D ... 27 D3
Nieder-Wöllstadt D 20 A3
Niederalteich D 28 C3
Niederau A 36 A3
Niederaula D 20 C4
Niederbronn-les-Bains F .. 25 E4
Niederkrüchten D 12 C2
Niederwinkling D 28 C3
Niemegk D 16 B3
Nienburg D 8 B1
Nienhagen D 10 A4
Nierstein D 19 F2
Niesky D 17 E1
Nieuweschans NL 7 E3
Nijkerk NL 6 B1
Nijmegen NL 12 B3
Nijverdal NL 7 D1
Nitra SK 31 F2
Nitrianske Pravno SK .. 31 F3
Nitrianske Rudno SK ... 31 F3
Nittenau D 28 B4
Nittendorf D 28 A3
Nivå DK 4 B4
Nogent F 24 A2
Nohfelden D 19 D2
Nomeny F 24 C4
Nomexy F 24 C3
Nonnenhorn D 34 B4
Noordwijk aan Zee NL .. 6 A1
Nordborg DK 3 D3
Nordby DK 2 B4
Norddeich D 7 E4
Norden D 7 E3
Nordenham D 8 B3
Norderney D 7 E4
Norderstedt D 9 D3
Nordhalben D 21 E3
Nordhausen D 15 D2
Nordhorn D 7 D1
Nördlingen D 27 D3
Nordskov DK 3 E4
Norg NL 7 D2
Nørre Åby DK 3 D4
Nørre Alslev DK 4 A2
Nørre Broby DK 3 D3
Nørre Lyndelse DK 3 E3
Nørre Nebel DK 2 B4
Norre Vejrup DK 2 C4
Nörten-Hardenberg D .. 14 C2
Northeim D 14 C2

Nortorf D 3 D1
Nossen D 22 C4
Nottuln D 13 E3
Nova H 38 C2
Nová Bystřice CZ 30 A3
Nova Levante/
Welschnofen I 35 E1
Nová Paka CZ 23 F3
Nováky SK 31 F3
Nové Hrady CZ 29 F3
Nové Město na
Moravě CZ 30 B4
Nové Mesto
nad Váhom SK 31 E3
Nové Sady SK 31 E2
Nové Strašeci CZ 23 D2
Nové Zámky SK 31 F1
Novi Marof HR 38 C1
Nový Bor CZ 23 E3
Nový Bydžov CZ 23 F2
Nový Jičín CZ 31 E4
Nový Knín CZ 23 D1
Nowe Warpno PL 11 E3
Nowogard PL 11 F3
Nowogród
Bobrzański PL 17 F2
Nowogrodziec PL 17 F1
Nozeroy F 32 B3
Nunsdorf D 16 C3
Nunspeet NL 6 C1
Nürburg D 19 D3
Nürnberg D 21 D1
Nürtingen D 26 B3
Nuttlar D 14 A2
Nyborg DK 3 E3
Nyby DK 4 B2
Nykøbing DK 4 A4
Nykøbing DK 4 A2
Nymburk CZ 23 E2
Nyon CH 32 B2
Nýrsko CZ 28 C4
Nysted DK 4 A2

O

Ober-Roden D 20 A2
Oberammergau D 35 E4
Oberau D 35 E4
Oberaudorf D 36 A4
Oberdrauburg A 36 C2
Obergrafendorf A 30 B1
Obergünzburg D 27 D1
Obergurgl A 35 E2
Oberhausen D 13 D2
Oberhof D 21 D4
Oberhofen CH 33 D3
Oberjoch D 35 D4
Oberkirch D 25 E3
Oberkochen D 26 C3
Obernai F 25 E3
Obernberg A 28 C2
Obernburg D 20 B2
Oberndorf A 28 C1
Oberndorf D 26 A2
Obernzell D 29 D2
Oberpullendorf A 38 C3
Oberriet CH 34 B3
Obersickte D 15 D3
Obersontheim D 26 C4
Oberstaufen D 34 C4
Oberstdorf D 34 C4
Obersuhl D 14 C1
Obertauern A 37 D3
Obertraubling D 28 B3
Obertraun A 37 D4
Obervellach A 36 C2
Oberviechtach D 22 A1
Oberwald CH 33 D2
Oberwart A 38 C3
Oberwesel D 19 E3
Oberwiesenthal D 22 B3

Oberwölz A 37 E3
Oberzeiring A 37 E3
Obing D 28 B1
Öblarn A 37 D3
Obsteig A 35 E3
Ochsenfurt D 20 C2
Ochsenhausen D 26 C2
Ochtrup D 13 E4
Odelzhausen D 27 E2
Odense DK 3 E3
Oderberg D 11 D1
Ødsted DK 2 C4
Oebisfelde D 15 E4
Oederan D 22 C4
Oeding D 13 D3
Oelde D 13 F3
Oelsnitz D 22 A3
Oettingen D 27 D3
Oetz A 35 D3
Offenbach D 20 A3
Offenburg D 25 E3
Ogenbargen D 7 F3
Ohrdruf D 21 D4
Öhringen D 26 C4
Oirschot NL 12 B3
Oisterwijk NL 12 A3
Oker D 15 D3
Oksböl DK 2 B4
Øksendrup DK 3 E3
Olbernhau D 22 C3
Oldenburg D 8 A2
Oldenburg D 3 E1
Oldenzaal NL 13 D4
Olivone CH 34 A2
Ollerup DK 3 E3
Olomouc CZ 31 D4
Olpe D 13 E1
Olsberg D 14 A2
Olst NL 6 C1
Olszyna PL 17 E2
Olszyna PL 23 F4
Olten CH 33 E4
Omegna I 33 E1
Ommen NL 7 D1
Oosterbeek NL 12 C4
Oostérend NL 6 B3
Oosterhout NL 12 A3
Oosterwolde NL 7 D2
Oostmalle B 12 A2
Ootmarsum NL 7 D1
Opařany CZ 29 E4
Opladen D 13 D2
Oppach D 23 E4
Oppenau D 25 F3
Oppenheim D 19 F2
Ora/Auer I 35 E1
Oranienbaum D 16 B2
Oranienburg D 10 C1
Ørbæk DK 3 E3
Orbe CH 32 B3
Orbey F 25 D2
Orehoved DK 4 A2
Orgelet F 32 A2
Öriszentpéter H 38 C2
Orlik nad Vltavou CZ 23 D1
Ormož SLO 38 C1
Ornans F 32 B4
Oron-la-Ville CH 32 C2
Oroszló H 39 F1
Orscholz D 18 C2
Orsières CH 32 C1
Ort A 28 C2
Ortenberg D 20 B3
Ortenburg D 28 C2
Orth A 30 C1
Ortisei/St Ulrich I 35 F2
Ortrand D 17 D1
Oschatz D 16 C1
Oschersleben D 15 E3
Osľany SK 31 F2
Osnabrück D 13 F4
Ośno PL 17 E4
Oss NL 12 B3
Ossiach A 37 D2

Ostbevern D 13 E3
Osted DK 4 B4
Osterburg D 9 F1
Osterburken D 20 B1
Osterhofen D 28 C3
Osterholz-Scharmbeck D 8 B2
Østerlars DK 5 F3
Østermarie DK 5 F3
Osterode D 15 D2
Ostheim D 20 C3
Osthofen D 19 F2
Ostrach D 26 B1
Ostritz D 23 E4
Ostrov CZ 22 B3
Osztopán H 39 E1
Otrokovice CZ 31 E4
Ottenschlag A 30 A2
Ottensheim A 29 E2
Otterbach D 19 E2
Otterlo NL 12 B4
Otterndorf D 8 B4
Ottersberg D 8 B2
Otterup DK 3 E4
Öttevény H 39 E4
Ottobeuren D 27 D1
Ottweiler D 19 D1
Oude-Pekela NL 7 E2
Ovelgönne D 8 C3
Ovenstädt D 14 B4
Over Jerstal DK 2 C3
Overath D 13 D1
Owschlag D 2 C1
Oyonnax F 32 A2
Oyten D 8 B2
Ožbalt SLO 38 A1

P

Pacov CZ 29 F4
Pacsa H 39 D2
Paderborn D 14 A3
Pagny F 24 B4
Paliseul B 18 A3
Paluzza I 36 C1
Pamhagen A 39 E4
Pápa H 39 E3
Papenburg D 7 E2
Pappenheim D 27 E3
Parchim D 10 A3
Parey D 16 A4
Parłówko PL 11 E3
Parpan CH 34 B2
Parsberg D 27 F4
Partenen A 34 C3
Partizánske SK 31 F2
Pasewalk D 11 D3
Pasiecznik PL 23 F4
Passau D 29 D2
Patergassen A 37 D2
Paternion A 37 D2
Patersdorf D 28 C3
Patsch A 35 E3
Pattensen D 14 C4
Payerne CH 32 C3
Peckelsheim D 14 B2
Pécsvárad H 39 F1
Pedráces/Pedratsches I 35 F2
Pedratsches/Pedráces I 35 F2
Peenemünde D 11 D4
Pegau D 16 A1
Peggau A 38 A3
Pegnitz D 21 E2
Peine D 15 D4
Peio I 35 D1
Peiss D 27 F1
Peissenberg D 27 E1
Peiting D 27 E1
Pelczyce PL 11 F1
Pelhřimov CZ 30 A4
Penkum D 11 E2

Penzberg D 35 E4
Penzlin D 10 C3
Perchtoldsdorf A 30 C1
Perg A 29 E2
Pèrgine Valsugana I 35 E1
Perleberg D 10 A2
Pernitz A 38 B4
Persenbeug A 29 F1
Pertisau A 35 F3
Pesmes F 32 A4
Pessin D 10 B1
Petange L 18 B2
Petersdorf D 3 E1
Petersdorf D 10 B4
Petershagen D 14 B4
Petkus D 16 C3
Petrovice CZ 23 D1
Pettenbach A 29 D1
Peuerbach A 29 D2
Pezinok SK 31 D2
Pfaffendorf D 21 D3
Pfaffenhausen D 27 D1
Pfaffenhofen D 27 F2
Pfaffikon CH 34 A3
Pfäffikon CH 34 A4
Pfafflar A 35 D3
Pfarrkirchen D 28 C2
Pfatter D 28 B3
Pfeffenhausen D 28 A3
Pforzheim D 26 A3
Pfreimd D 22 A1
Pfronten D 35 D4
Pfullendorf D 26 B1
Pfullingen D 26 B3
Pfunds A 35 D3
Pfungstadt D 19 F2
Phalsbourg F 25 D3
Philippsreut D 29 D3
Philippsthal D 20 C4
Piechowice PL 23 F4
Pierrefitte I 24 A4
Pieski PL 17 F4
Piešťany SK 31 E2
Pieve di Cadore I 36 A1
Pincehely H 39 F2
Pinkafeld A 38 B3
Pinneberg D 8 C3
Pinzolo I 35 D1
Piotta CH 33 F2
Pirmasens D 19 D1
Pirna D 23 D4
Písek CZ 29 E4
Planá CZ 22 B2
Planá nad Lužnicí CZ 29 F4
Plánice CZ 29 D4
Plansee A 35 D4
Plasy CZ 22 C2
Plattling D 28 C3
Plau D 10 B3
Plaue D 16 B4
Plauen D 22 A3
Plech D 21 E1
Pleinfeld D 27 E4
Plettenberg D 13 E2
Plochingen D 26 B3
Plombières-sur-Bains F 24 C2
Plön D 3 D1
Ploty PL 11 F3
Plzeň CZ 22 C1
Pobierowo PL 11 F4
Počátky CZ 30 A4
Pöchlarn A 30 A1
Pocking D 28 C2
Podbořany CZ 22 C2
Poděbrady CZ 23 F2
Podersdorf am See A 39 E4
Podivín CZ 31 D3
Podkoren SLO 37 D1
Poggendorf D 10 C4
Pohořelice CZ 30 C3
Poissons F 24 A3
Polgárdi H 39 F2
Police PL 11 E3
Poligny F 32 A3

Polle D 14 B3
Pomellen D 11 E2
Pomezí nad Ohří CZ 22 A2
Pommersfelden D 21 D2
Pompaples CH 32 B3
Pompey F 24 B4
Pont-à-Mousson F 24 B4
Pont-de-Roide F 32 C4
Pont-St-Vincent F 24 B3
Pontailler-sur-Saône F 32 A4
Pontarlier F 32 B3
Ponte Arche I 35 D1
Ponte di Legno I 35 D1
Ponte nelle Alpi I 36 A1
Ponte Tresa CH 33 F1
Pontebba I 36 C1
Pontresina CH 34 C2
Poppenhausen D 20 C2
Pörnbach D 27 F3
Porrentruy CH 33 D4
Port-sur-Saône F 24 B1
Pörtschach A 37 D2
Poschiavo CH 34 C1
Pössneck D 21 F4
Postoloprty CZ 22 C3
Potsdam D 16 C4
Pottenstein A 30 B1
Pottenstein D 21 E2
Pöttmes D 27 E3
Považská Bystrica SK 31 F3
Poysdorf A 30 C2
Pożrzadło PL 17 F3
Prachatice CZ 29 D3
Prägraten A 36 B3
Praha CZ 23 E2
Præstø DK 4 B3
Prauthoy F 24 A2
Pravlov CZ 30 C3
Pré St-Didier I 32 C1
Predazzo I 35 E1
Preddvor SLO 37 E1
Predel SLO 37 D1
Predlitz A 37 D3
Predoi/Prettau I 36 A3
Preetz D 3 D1
Pregarten A 29 E2
Přelouč CZ 23 F2
Přemnitz D 16 B4
Prenzlau D 11 D2
Přerov CZ 31 E4
Prerow D 4 B1
Pressath D 21 F2
Pressbaum A 30 B1
Přeštice CZ 22 C1
Prettau/Predoi I 36 A3
Prettin D 16 B2
Pretzsch D 16 B2
Přibeta SK 31 F1
Příbor CZ 31 F4
Příbram CZ 23 D1
Přibyslav CZ 30 B4
Prichsenstadt D 20 C2
Prien D 28 B1
Primda CZ 22 B1
Primstal D 18 C2
Pritzerbe D 16 B4
Pritzier D 9 E3
Pritzwalk D 10 B2
Probstzella D 21 E3
Pronsfeld D 18 C3
Prostějov CZ 31 D4
Protivín CZ 29 E4
Prötzel D 17 D4
Prüm D 18 C3
Prunn D 27 F3
Przybiernów PL 11 E3
Ptuj SLO 38 B1
Puchberg A 38 B4
Púchov SK 31 F3
Puffendorf D 12 C1
Pulkau A 30 B2
Pulsnitz D 17 D1
Purbach A 38 C4
Purgstall A 30 A1

53

Purkersdorf A 30 C1
Purmerend NL 6 A2
Pusztaszemes H 39 E2
Putbus D 5 D1
Putim CZ 29 E4
Putlitz D 10 A2
Puttelange F 25 D4
Putten NL 6 B1
Puttgarden D 3 F1
Pyrzyce PL 11 E2
Pyšely CZ 23 E2

Q

Quakenbrück D 7 F1
Quedlinburg D 15 E3
Querfurt D 15 F2
Quickborn D 9 D3
Quingey F 32 B4

R

Raab A 29 D2
Raabs an der Thaya A 30 A3
Raalte NL 6 C1
Rábafüzes H 38 C2
Rabí CZ 29 D4
Rača SK 31 D1
Rade D 8 C3
Radeberg D 17 D1
Radebeul D 16 C1
Radeburg D 17 D1
Radegast D 16 A2
Radenci SLO 38 B2
Radenthein A 37 D2
Radevormwald D 13 D2
Radkersburg A 38 B2
Radlje ob Dráwi SLO 38 A2
Radmirje SLO 37 F1
Radnica PL 17 F3
Radnice CZ 22 C2
Radolfzell D 26 A1
Radošina SK 31 E2
Radošovce SK 31 D3
Radotín CZ 23 D2
Radovljica SLO 37 D1
Radstadt A 36 C3
Raesfeld D 13 D3
Ragaška Slatina SLO 38 B1
Rahden D 14 A4
Rain D 27 E3
Rajec SK 31 F3
Rajka H 31 D1
Rakovník CZ 22 C2
Rambervillers F 24 C3
Rambin D 4 C1
Ramsau A 37 D3
Ramstein D 19 D1
Ranalt A 35 E3
Rankweil A 34 B3
Raon-l'Etape F 25 D3
Rapperswil CH 34 A3
Raron CH 33 D2
Rastatt D 25 F3
Rastede D 8 A3
Rastenfeld A 30 A2
Ratece SLO 37 D1
Ratekau D 9 E4
Rathenow D 16 B4
Ratingen D 13 D2
Ratten A 38 B3
Rattenberg A 36 A3
Rattersdorf A 38 C3
Ratzeburg D 9 E3
Raubling D 36 A4
Rauris A 36 C3
Ravensbrück D 10 C2
Ravensburg D 26 C1

Realp CH 33 F2
Rechnitz A 38 C3
Recke D 13 E4
Recklinghausen D 13 D3
Recologne F 32 A4
Recz PL 11 F2
Redefin D 9 E2
Rédics H 38 C1
Rees D 12 C3
Regen D 28 C3
Regensburg D 28 A3
Regenstauf D 28 A4
Rehau D 21 F3
Rehden D 8 A1
Rehna D 9 E3
Reichenau an der Rax A ... 38 B4
Reichenbach D 22 A3
Reichenbach D 17 E1
Reichertshausen D 27 F2
Reichertshofen D 27 F3
Reignier F 32 B2
Reinach CH 33 D4
Reinach CH 33 E3
Reinberg D 10 C4
Reinfeld D 9 E4
Reinhardshagen D 14 C2
Reinheim D 20 A2
Reinsfeld D 18 C2
Reisbach D 28 B2
Reischach D 28 B2
Reischenhart D 36 A4
Reit im Winkl D 36 B4
Reitzehain D 22 C3
Rejštejn CZ 29 D4
Reken D 13 D3
Remagen D 19 D4
Remels D 7 F3
Remich L 18 B2
Remiremont F 24 C2
Remouchamps B 18 B4
Remscheid D 13 D2
Renchen D 25 E3
Rendsburg D 2 C1
Renkum NL 12 B4
Rennerod D 19 E4
Rennweg A 37 D2
Rens DK 2 C3
Répcelak H 39 D3
Rerik D 10 A4
Resko PL 11 F3
Rethem D 8 C1
Retz A 30 B3
Reusel NL 12 A3
Reuterstadt
  Stavenhagen D 10 C3
Reutlingen D 26 B3
Reutte A 35 D4
Revfülöp H 39 E2
Révigny F 24 A4
Řevničov CZ 23 D2
Rewal PL 11 F4
Rheda D 13 F3
Rhede D 13 D3
Rheinau D 25 E3
Rheinbach D 19 D4
Rheinberg D 12 C3
Rheinböllen D 19 E3
Rheindahlen D 12 C2
Rheine D 13 E4
Rheinfelden CH 25 E1
Rheinfelden D 25 E1
Rheinsberg D 10 C2
Rheinzabern D 25 F4
Rhenen NL 12 B4
Rhens D 19 E3
Rheydt D 12 C2
Rhinau F 25 E2
Rhinow D 10 B1
Rhynern D 13 E3
Riale I 33 E2
Ribe DK 2 B3
Ribeauville F 25 D2
Ribnitz-Damgarten D 4 B1
Říčany CZ 23 E2

Richtenberg D 10 C4
Rickling D 9 D4
Ried A 35 D3
Ried im Innkreis A 29 D2
Riedenburg D 27 F3
Riedlingen D 26 B2
Riegel D 25 E2
Riegersburg A 38 B2
Riesa D 16 C1
Riestedt D 15 E2
Rietberg D 14 A3
Riezlern A 34 C3
Rijssen NL 7 D1
Ringe DK 3 E3
Ringsted DK 4 A3
Rinteln D 14 B4
Rioz F 24 B1
Riquewihr F 25 D2
Risnovce SK 31 E2
Ristinge DK 3 E2
Risum-Lindholm D 2 B2
Rittmanshausen D 14 C1
Röbel D 10 B2
Rochefort B 18 A3
Rochefort-s-Nenon F 32 A4
Rochlitz D 22 B4
Rockenhausen D 19 E2
Rodach D 21 D3
Rødby DK 3 F2
Rødbyhavn DK 3 F2
Rødding DK 2 C4
Rødekro DK 2 C3
Roden NL 7 D3
Rodenkirchen D 8 A3
Rodewald D 8 C1
Rodewisch D 22 A3
Roding D 28 B4
Rødvig DK 4 B3
Roermond NL 12 B2
Rogatec SLO 38 B1
Rogätz D 15 F4
Rohrbach A 29 D2
Rohrbach lès Bitche F 25 D4
Rohrberg D 9 E1
Rokycany CZ 22 C1
Rolle CH 32 B2
Romanshorn CH 34 B4
Rombas F 18 B1
Romont CH 32 C3
Roncegno I 35 E1
Ronchamp F 24 C1
Rønne DK 5 E3
Ronneburg D 22 A4
Ronnede DK 4 B3
Roodeschool NL 7 D3
Rorschach CH 34 B4
Rørvig DK 4 A4
Rosche D 9 E2
Rosegg A 37 D1
Rosenheim D 28 A1
Rosice CZ 30 C3
Roskilde DK 4 B4
Rosshaupten D 35 D4
Rossla D 15 E2
Rosslau D 16 A3
Röstånga S 4 C4
Rostock D 10 B4
Rotenburg D 14 C1
Rotenburg D 8 C2
Roth D 27 E4
Rötha D 16 B1
Rothenburg D 17 E1
Rothenburg ob
  der Tauber D 20 C1
Rott D 27 E1
Rott D 28 A1
Rottach D 35 F4
Rottenbach D 21 D3
Rottenburg D 26 B3
Rottenburg D 28 A3
Rottenmann A 37 E3
Rotthalmünster D 28 C2
Röttingen D 20 C1
Rottweil D 26 A2

Rötz D 28 B4
Roudnice n Labem CZ 23 D3
Rouffach F 25 D2
Rougemont F 24 B1
Rougemont F 24 C1
Rouvres-en-Xaintois F 24 B3
Rövershagen D 10 B4
Rów PL 11 E1
Różanki PL 11 F1
Rožmitál pod
  Třemšínen CZ 23 D1
Rožnov pod
  Radhoštěm CZ 31 F4
Rozvadov CZ 22 B1
Rudawica PL 17 F2
Rüdesheim D 19 E3
Rudkøbing DK 3 E2
Rudolphstein D 21 F3
Rudolstadt D 21 E4
Ruds-Vedby DK 3 F4
Ruffieux F 32 A1
Rühen D 15 E4
Ruhland D 17 D2
Ruhmannsfelden D 28 C3
Ruhpolding D 36 B4
Rülzheim D 25 F4
Rum H 39 D3
Rumburk CZ 23 E4
Rumilly F 32 A1
Rupt F 24 C2
Rüsselsheim D 19 F2
Rust A 38 C4
Rust D 25 E2
Ruswil CH 33 E3
Rutenbrock D 7 E2
Rüthen D 14 A2
Rüti CH 34 A3
Ruurlo NL 12 C4
Ruwer D 18 C2
Rysum D 7 E3
Rzepin PL 17 E3

S

Saal D 28 A3
Saalbach A 36 B3
Saales F 25 D3
Saalfeld D 21 E3
Saalfelden A 36 B3
Saanen CH 33 D2
Saarbrücken D 18 C1
Saarburg D 18 C2
Saarlouis D 18 C1
Saas-Fee CH 33 E1
Sæd DK 2 C3
Sądów PL 17 E3
Sadská CZ 23 E2
Saerbeck D 13 E4
Saeul L 18 B2
Sagard D 5 D1
Ságvár H 39 F2
Saignelégier CH 32 C4
St Aegyd A 38 B4
St-Amé F 24 C2
St Andrä A 37 F2
St Andreasberg D 15 D2
St Annaparochie NL 6 C3
St Anton A 34 C3
St-Avold F 18 C1
St Blasien D 25 E1
St-Blin F 24 A3
St-Cergue CH 32 B2
St Christina/
  Santa Cristina I 35 F2
St Christoph A 34 C3
St-Claude F 32 A2
St-Dié F 25 D3
St-Dizier F 24 A4
St Englmar D 28 C3
St Gallen A 37 E4
St Gallen CH 34 B4

St Gallenkirch A 34 C3
St-Genix-sur-Guiers F 32 A1
St Georgen A 28 C1
St Georgen A 37 E3
St Georgen D 25 F2
St-Germain-de-Joux F 32 A2
St-Gervais-les-Bains F 32 B1
St Gilgen A 36 C4
St Gingolph CH 32 C2
St Goar D 19 E3
St Goarshausen D 19 E3
St-Gorgon-Main F 32 B3
St-Hippolyte F 32 C4
St-Hubert B 18 A3
St-Imier CH 32 C4
St Ingbert D 19 D1
St Jakob im Rosental A 37 D1
St-Jeoire F 32 B2
St Johann am Tauern A 37 E3
St Johann im Pongau A 36 C3
St Johann in Tirol A 36 B4
St-Jorioz F 32 B1
St-Julien-en-Genevois F 32 A2
St Lambrecht A 37 E2
St-Laurent-en-
   Grandvaux F 32 A3
St Leonhard A 30 A1
St Lorenzen A 36 B2
St-Louis F 25 D1
St-Loup-sur-Semouse F 24 B2
St Luc CH 33 D1
St Märgen D 25 E2
St-Maurice CH 32 C2
St Maurice-sur-Moselle F 24 C2
St Michael A 37 D3
St Michael A 37 F3
St Michael A 38 C3
St-Mihiel F 24 B4
St Moritz CH 34 C2
St Nicolas-de-Port F 24 C3
St Niklaus I 33 D1
St Nikolai A 37 D3
St Oedenrode NL 12 B3
St Olof S 5 E4
St Oswald A 29 E2
St Paul A 37 F2
St Peter-Ording D 2 B1
St Pötten A 30 B1
St-Thiébault F 24 A3
St-Truiden B 12 A1
St Ulrich/Ortisei I 35 F2
St Valentin A 29 E1
St Veit A 37 E2
St-Vestec CZ 23 E2
St Vigil/San Vigilio I 35 F2
St Vith B 18 B3
St Wendel D 19 D2
St Wolfgang A 36 C4
Ste-Croix CH 32 B3
Ste-Marie-aux-Mines F 25 D2
Sakskøbing DK 4 A2
Šal'a SK 31 E1
Salem D 26 B1
Salins F 32 A3
Sallanches F 32 B1
Saltbæk DK 3 F4
Sælvig DK 3 E4
Salzburg A 36 C4
Salzgitter-Bad D 15 D3
Salzgitter-Lebenstedt D 15 D3
Salzhausen D 9 D2
Salzkotten D 14 A3
Salzwedel D 9 E1
Salzweg D 29 D2
Samedan CH 34 C2
Samoëns F 32 C1
Šamorin SK 31 D1
Samtens D 4 C1
San Bernardino CH 34 B2
San Candido/Innichen I 36 A2
San Daniele del Friuli I 36 B1
San Leonardo in Passiria I .. 35 E2
San Martino di
   Castrozza I 35 F1

San Michele all'Adige I 35 E1
San Stéfano di Cadore I 36 B2
San Valentino alla Muta I .. 35 D2
San Vigilio/St Vigil I 35 F2
San Vito di Cadore I 36 A1
Sand in Taufers/
   Campo Tures I 35 F2
Sandau D 10 A1
Sande D 8 A3
Sandl A 29 E2
Sandstedt D 8 B3
Sandvig DK 5 E3
Sangerhausen D 15 E2
Sanitz D 10 B4
Sankt-Michaelisdonn D 8 C4
Sannenmöser CH 33 D2
Santa Caterina Valfurva I .. 35 D1
Santa Cristina/
   St Christina I 35 F2
Santa Maria Maggiore I 33 E1
Santok PL 11 F1
Sappada I 36 B2
Sappemeer NL 7 D3
Sarbinowo PL 17 E4
Sarentino-Sarntal I 35 E2
Sargans CH 34 B3
Sárkeresztúr H 39 F2
Sarnen CH 33 E3
Sarralbe F 25 D4
Sarre-Union F 25 D4
Sarrebourg F 25 D3
Sarreguemines F 18 C1
Sarstedt D 14 C4
Sárvár H 39 D3
Sásd H 39 F1
Sassenberg D 13 F3
Sassenheim NL 6 A1
Sassnitz D 5 D1
Šaštín- Stráže SK 31 D2
Satow D 10 A4
Satrup D 2 C2
Sauerlach D 27 F1
Saulgau D 26 B2
Saulx F 24 B1

Saulxures F 24 C2
Saverne F 25 D3
Savognin CH 34 B2
Schaan FL 34 B3
Schachendorf A 38 C3
Schaffhausen CH 26 A1
Schafstädt D 15 F2
Schäftlam D 27 E1
Schagen NL 6 A2
Scharbeutz D 9 E4
Schärding A 28 C2
Scharnitz A 35 E3
Scharnstein A 29 D1
Scheer D 26 B2
Scheessel D 8 C2
Scheibbs A 30 A1
Scheifling A 37 E3
Scheinfeld D 21 D1
Schenefeld D 8 C4
Scherfede D 14 B2
Schermbeck D 13 D3
Schesslitz D 21 E2
Scheyern D 27 F2
Schieder D 14 B3
Schierling D 28 A3
Schiermonnikoog NL 6 C3
Schifferstadt D 19 F1
Schilpário I 34 C1
Schiltach D 25 F2
Schirmeck F 25 D3
Schirnding D 22 A2
Schkeuditz D 16 A2
Schladen D 15 D3
Schladming A 37 D3
Schlanders/Silandro I 35 D2
Schlangenbad D 19 E3
Schleching D 36 B4
Schleiden D 18 C4
Schleiz D 21 F3
Schleswig D 2 C2
Schleusingen D 21 D3
Schlieben D 16 C2
Schliersee D 35 F4
Schlitz D 20 B4

Schlotheim D 15 D1
Schluchsee D 25 E1
Schlüchtern D 20 B3
Schluderns/Sluderno I 35 D2
Schludersbach/
   Carbonin I 36 A2
Schlüsselfeld D 21 D2
Schlutup D 9 E4
Schmalkalden D 21 D4
Schmallenberg D 13 F2
Schmidmühlen D 28 A4
Schmilka D 23 D4
Schmölln D 22 A4
Schmölln D 11 D2
Schnackenburg D 9 F2
Schnaittenbach D 21 F1
Schneeberg D 22 B3
Schneverdingen D 8 C2
Schöder A 37 D3
Schöllkrippen D 20 B3
Schönau D 25 E1
Schönbeck D 11 D3
Schönberg A 35 E3
Schönberg D 3 D1
Schönberg D 9 E3
Schönberg D 9 C3
Schönberg D 28 A2
Schönberg D 28 C3
Schönbergerstrand D 3 E1
Schönebeck D 15 F3
Schönebeck D 10 B2
Schönecken D 18 C3
Schongau D 27 E1
Schönhagen D 3 D2
Schöningen D 15 E3
Schönthal D 28 B4
Schönwald D 25 F2
Schönwalde D 3 E1
Schönwalde D 10 C1
Schoonebeek NL 7 D2
Schoonhoven NL 12 A4
Schoonoord NL 7 D2
Schopfheim D 25 E1
Schöppenstedt D 15 E3
Schoppernau A 34 C3

55

Schorndorf D	26	C3
Schotten D	20	B3
Schramberg D	25	F2
Schrems A	29	F3
Schriesheim D	19	F1
Schrobenhausen D	27	E2
Schröcken A	34	C3
Schruns A	34	C3
Schüpfheim CH	33	E3
Schüttorf D	13	E4
Schwaan D	10	B4
Schwabach D	27	E4
Schwabhausen D	27	E2
Schwäbisch Gmünd D	26	C3
Schwäbisch Hall D	26	C4
Schwabmünchen D	27	D2
Schwaigern D	26	B4
Schwalenberg D	14	B3
Schwalmstadt-Treysa D	14	B1
Schwalmstadt-Ziegenhain D	14	B1
Schwanden CH	34	A3
Schwandorf D	28	A4
Schwanebeck D	15	E3
Schwanewede D	8	B2
Schwaney D	14	B3
Schwarmstedt D	8	C1
Schwarzach A	36	C3
Schwarzenbach D	21	F3
Schwarzenbek D	9	D3
Schwarzenberg D	22	B3
Schwarzenfeld D	28	B4
Schwarzsee CH	33	D2
Schwaz A	35	F3
Schwechat A	30	C1
Schwedt D	11	E2
Schweich D	18	C2
Schweinfurt D	20	C2
Schwelm D	13	D2
Schwenningen D	25	F2
Schwerin D	9	F3
Schwerte D	13	E2
Schwetzingen D	19	F1
Schwyz CH	33	F3
Scuol CH	34	C2
Sebnitz D	23	D4
Seč CZ	22	C1
Seč CZ	23	F2
Seckau A	37	F3
Sédico I	36	A1
Sedlčany CZ	23	D1
Sedlice CZ	29	D4
Sedrun CH	33	F2
Seeboden A	36	C2
Seebruck D	28	B1
Seefeld in Tyrol A	35	E3
Seehausen D	15	E3
Seehausen D	10	A1
Seehausen D	16	B3
Seelbach D	25	E2
Seelow D	17	E4
Seeon D	28	B1
Seesen D	15	D3
Seeshaupt D	27	E1
Seewalchen A	29	D1
Seewiesen A	38	A4
Segesd H	39	D1
Sehnde D	14	C4
Seifhannersdorf D	23	E4
Seitenstetten A	29	E1
Selb D	22	A2
Selent D	3	E1
Sélestat F	25	D2
Sellières F	32	A3
Sellin D	5	D1
Selm D	13	E3
Selmsdorf D	9	E4
Selongey F	24	A1
Selsingen D	8	C3
Seltz F	25	F4
Selva di Val Gardena/Wolkenstein in Gardena I	35	F2
Semily CZ	23	F3
Semmering A	38	B4
Senden D	13	E3
Sendenhorst D	13	E3
Senec SK	31	E1
Senftenberg D	17	D2
Senica SK	31	D2
Sennelager D	14	A3
Sennestadt D	14	A3
Senones F	25	D3
Sentilj SLO	38	B2
Seraing B	12	B1
Sered' SK	31	E2
Serfaus A	35	D3
Sermaize-les-Bains F	24	A4
Sesto/Sexten I	36	A2
Severin D	10	A3
Ševětín CZ	29	E3
Sevrier F	32	A1
Sexten/Sesto I	36	A2
Seyda D	16	B3
Seyssel F	32	A1
Sezimovo Ústí CZ	29	F4
Siddeburen NL	7	D3
Siegburg D	13	D1
Siegen D	13	E1
Siegenburg D	28	A3
Sieggraben A	38	C4
Siegsdorf D	36	B4
Siekierki PL	11	E1
Sieniawka PL	23	E4
Sierck-les-Bains F	18	B2
Sierentz F	25	D1
Sierning A	29	E1
Sierre CH	33	D2
Sigmaringen D	26	B2
Silandro/Schlanders I	35	D2
Silberstedt D	2	C2
Sillian A	36	B2
Sils-Maria CH	34	B2
Silvaplana CH	34	B2
Silz A	35	D3
Simaság H	39	D3
Simbach D	28	B2
Simbach D	28	C2
Simmerath D	18	C4
Simmerberg D	34	C4
Simmern D	19	D3
Simplon Dorf CH	33	E1
Simrishamn S	5	E3
Sindelfingen D	26	B3
Singen D	26	A1
Sinsheim D	20	A1
Sinzig D	19	D4
Siófok H	39	F2
Sion CH	33	D2
Sirnach CH	34	A4
Sissach CH	33	E4
Sittard NL	12	B2
Sittensen D	8	C2
Siusi I	35	E2
Sjöbo S	5	D4
Skalica SK	31	D3
Skælskør DK	3	F3
Skanör S	4	C3
Skąpe PL	17	F3
Skærbæk DK	2	B3
Skårup DK	3	E3
Skelde DK	3	D2
Skibby DK	4	B4
Skillinge S	5	E3
Škofja Loka SLO	37	E1
Skovballe DK	3	E3
Skovby DK	3	D2
Skurup S	5	D3
Skwierzyna PL	17	F4
Sládkovičovo SK	31	E1
Slagelse DK	3	F3
Slangerup DK	4	B4
Slaný CZ	23	D2
Slavonice CZ	30	A3
Sliedrecht NL	12	A4
Słońsk PL	17	E4
Sloten NL	6	C2
Slovenj Gradec SLO	37	F1
Slovenska Bistrica SLO	38	B1
Slovenske Konjice SLO	38	A1
Słubice PL	17	E3
Sluderno/Schluderns I	35	D2
Smědeč CZ	29	E3
Smidary CZ	23	F2
Smilde NL	7	D2
Smygehamn S	5	D3
Snaptun DK	3	D4
Snarup DK	3	E3
Sneek NL	6	C3
Snøde DK	3	E3
Snogebaek DK	5	F2
Soběslav CZ	29	F4
Sobotište SK	31	E3
Sobotka CZ	23	F3
Søby DK	3	D2
Soest D	13	F2
Soest NL	12	B4
Soestdijk NL	6	B1
Sögel D	7	E2
Sokolov CZ	22	B2
Solda/Sulden I	35	D2
Sölden A	35	E3
Solingen D	13	D2
Söll A	36	A4
Sollenau A	38	C4
Søllested DK	3	F2
Sološnica SK	31	D2
Solothurn CH	33	D4
Solrød Strand DK	4	B4
Soltau D	8	C2
Sömmerda D	15	E1
Sommersted DK	2	C3
Somogyszob H	39	D1
Sonceboz CH	33	D4
Sóndalo I	34	C1
Sønderborg DK	3	D3
Sonderby DK	3	D2
Sønderho DK	2	B4
Sondershausen D	15	E2
Sønderso DK	3	E4
Sondrio I	34	B1
Sonneberg D	21	E3
Sonogno CH	33	F2
Sonsbeck D	12	C3
Sonthofen D	34	C4
Sontra D	14	C1
Sopron H	38	C4
Söréd H	39	F3
Sorø DK	4	A3
Sörup D	3	D2
Sottrum D	8	C2
Soufflenheim F	25	E3
Souilly F	18	A1
Soultz F	25	D2
Soultz F	25	E4
Sövestad S	5	D3
Spa B	18	B4
Spaichingen D	26	A2
Spakenburg NL	6	B1
Spálené Pořičí CZ	22	C1
Spalt D	27	E4
Spandau D	16	C4
Spangenberg D	14	C1
Speyer D	19	F1
Spiegelau D	28	C3
Spiekeroog D	7	F4
Spielfeld A	38	B2
Spiez CH	33	D2
Spilimbergo I	36	B1
Spincourt F	18	A2
Špindlerův-Mlýn CZ	23	F3
Spital am Pyhrn A	37	E4
Spittal an der Drau A	36	C2
Spitz A	30	A2
Splügen CH	34	B2
Spodsbjerg DK	3	E2
Sprakensehl D	9	D1
Spremberg D	17	E2
Springe D	14	C4
Staaken D	16	C4
Stachy CZ	29	D3
Stade D	8	C3
Stadskanaal NL	7	D2
Stadt Allendorf D	20	B4
Stadthagen D	14	B4
Stadtilm D	21	E4
Stadtkyll D	18	C4
Stadtlauringen D	21	D3
Stadtlohn D	13	D4
Stadtoldendorf D	14	C3
Stadtroda D	21	F4
Stadtsteinach D	21	E2
Staffelstein D	21	E2
Stahle D	14	B3
Stainach A	37	D3
Stainville F	24	A4
Stainz A	38	A2
Stalden CH	33	E1
Stams A	35	E3
Staňkov CZ	22	B1
Stans CH	33	F3
Stansstad CH	33	F3
Stare Czarnowo PL	11	E2
Staré Město CZ	31	E3
Stargard-Szczeciński PL	11	F2
Starnberg D	27	E1
Starogard PL	11	F3
Starup DK	2	C4
Starý Hrozenkov CZ	31	E3
Stavelot B	18	B4
Staveren NL	6	B2
Stechelberg CH	33	E2
Štěchovice CZ	23	D2
Steckborn CH	26	A1
Steeg A	34	C3
Steenwijk NL	6	C2
Stege DK	4	B2
Stegersbach A	38	C3
Stein am Rhein CH	26	A1
Steinach A	35	E3
Steinau D	20	B3
Steinberg D	3	D2
Steinfeld A	36	C2
Steinfeld D	8	A1
Steingaden D	35	D4
Steinhausen D	26	C2
Steinheim D	14	B3
Steinhorst D	9	D1
Stenay F	18	A2
Stendal D	16	A4
Stenlille DK	4	A4
Stenstrup DK	3	E3
Sternberg D	10	A3
Sterzing/Vipiteno I	35	E2
Štětí CZ	23	D3
Steyr A	29	E1
Steyrermühl A	29	D1
Stiens NL	6	C3
Štitary CZ	30	B3
Stockach D	26	B1
Stockelsdorf D	9	E4
Stockerau A	30	C2
Stockheim D	21	E3
Stod CZ	22	C1
Stokkemarke DK	3	F2
Štoky CZ	23	F1
Stolberg D	12	C1
Stollberg D	22	B3
Stolpe D	16	C4
Stolzenau D	8	B1
Stonařov CZ	30	B4
Store Darum DK	2	B4
Store Heddinge DK	4	B3
Store Merløse DK	4	A4
Storkow D	17	D3
Stotel D	8	B3
Stotternheim D	15	E1
Stouby DK	3	D4
Straach D	16	B3
Straelen D	12	C3
Strakonice CZ	29	D4
Stralsund D	4	C1
Strande D	3	D1
Stráni CZ	31	E3
Stranice SLO	38	A1

Strasbourg F 25 E3
Strasburg D 11 D3
Strassburg A 37 E2
Strassfurt D 15 F3
Strasswalchen A 28 C1
Straubing D 28 B3
Straupitz D 17 D3
Strausberg D 17 D3
Straussfurt D 15 E1
Strážnice CZ 31 D3
Strážný CZ 29 D3
Strehla D 16 C1
Streitberg D 21 E2
Strengberg A 29 E1
Stresa I 33 F1
Strib DK 3 D4
Stříbro CZ 22 B1
Strmilov CZ 30 A3
Strobl A 36 C4
Strøby Egede DK 4 B3
Stromberg D 19 E2
Strücklingen D 7 F2
Strzelce Krajeńskie PL 11 F1
Stubbekøbing DK 4 B2
Stuben A 34 C3
Stuckenborstel D 8 C2
Studánky CZ 29 E2
Studená CZ 30 A3
Stühlingen D 25 F1
Stukenbrock D 14 A3
Stülpe D 16 C3
Stupava SK 31 D2
Stuttgart D 26 B3
Suchań PL 11 F2
Suchdol nad
    Lužnici CZ 29 F3
Süchteln D 12 C2
Süden D 2 B2
Süderbrarup D 3 D2
Süderlugum D 2 C3
Suhl D 21 D3
Sulden/Solda I 35 D2
Sulęin PL 17 F4
Sulingen D 8 B1
Sulz D 26 A2
Sulzbach D 26 C4
Sulzbach-Rosenberg D 21 F1
Sümeg H 39 D2
Sumiswald CH 33 E3
Sundern D 13 F2
Šurany SK 31 F1
Sursee CH 33 E3
Susch CH 34 C2
Sušice CZ 29 D4
Süssen D 26 C3
Svaneke DK 5 F3
Sväty Jur SK 31 D2
Svedala S 4 C3
Svendborg DK 3 E3
Švermov CZ 23 D2
Světlá nad Sázavou CZ 23 F1
Švihov CZ 22 C1
Svinninge DK 4 A4
Swalmen NL 12 C2
Świdnica PL 17 F2
Świebodzin PL 17 F3
Świecko PL 17 E3
Świeradów-Zdrój PL 23 F4
Świerzno D 11 E3
Świnoujście PL 11 E3
Syke D 8 B2
Sylt Ost D 2 B3
Szakály H 39 F1
Szany H 39 D3
Szczecin PL 11 E2
Székesfehérvár H 39 F3
Szentlászló H 39 F4
Szil H 39 D3
Szklarska Poreba PL 23 F4
Szombathely H 38 C3
Szőny H 39 F4
Szprotawa PL 17 F2
's Heerenberg NL 12 C3
's-Hertogen-Bosch NL 12 B3

T

Tábor CZ 29 E4
Tachov CZ 22 B2
Tai di Cadore I 36 A1
Tailfingen D 26 B2
Takácsi H 39 E3
Talloires F 32 B1
Tamási H 39 F2
Tamsweg A 37 D3
Tangerhütte D 16 A4
Tangermünde D 16 A4
Taninges F 32 B1
Tann D 20 C4
Tanna D 15 D2
Tannheim A 35 D4
Tanvald CZ 16 D3
Tapolca H 39 E2
Tapolcafő H 39 E3
Taps DK 2 C4
Tarasp CH 34 C2
Tårbæk DK 4 B4
Tarcento I 36 C1
Tarmstedt D 8 B2
Tarp D 2 C2
Tars DK 3 E2
Tarvisio I 37 D1
Täsch CH 33 D1
Tåstrup DK 4 B4
Tata H 39 F4
Tatabánya H 39 F3
Tauberbischofsheim D 20 B2
Taucha D 16 B2
Taufers/Tubre I 35 D2
Taufkirchen A 28 B1
Taufkirchen D 28 A2
Taunusstein D 19 E3
Tauplitz A 37 D4
Tavannes CH 33 D4
Tavaux F 32 A4
Taxenbach A 36 C3
Techendorf A 36 C2
Tecklenburg D 13 E4
Tegelen NL 12 C2
Tegernsee D 35 F4
Teichel D 21 E4
Teisendorf D 28 B1
Telč CZ 30 A3
Telfs A 35 E3
Telgte D 13 E3
Tellingstedt D 2 C1
Templin D 10 C2
Teplá CZ 22 B2
Teplice CZ 23 D3
Ter Apel NL 7 E2
Terezin CZ 23 D3
Ternitz A 38 B4
Terz A 37 D4
Tessin D 10 B4
Tét H 39 E3
Teterow D 10 B3
Tettnang D 26 B1
Teufen CH 34 B4
Teupitz D 17 D3
Thale D 15 E2
Thalfang D 18 C2
Thalmässing D 27 E4
Thalwil CH 33 F4
Thann F 25 D2
Thannhausen D 27 D2
Tharandt D 22 C4
Themar D 21 D3
Theux B 18 B4
Thiaucourt-Regnéville F ... 24 B4
Thiendorf D 17 D1
Thiersee A 36 A4
Thiessow D 5 D1
Thionville F 18 B2
Tholey D 18 C2
Thonon F 32 B2
Thum D 22 B3

Thun CH 33 D3
Thürkow D 10 B3
Thurnau D 21 E2
Thusis CH 34 B2
Tiefencastel CH 34 B2
Tiefensee D 17 D4
Tiel NL 12 B4
Tienen B 12 A1
Tiengen D 25 F1
Tihany H 39 E2
Tilburg NL 12 A3
Timmendorfer Strand D ... 9 E4
Tinglev DK 2 C3
Tione di Trento I 35 D1
Tirano I 34 C1
Tirschenreuth D 22 A2
Tišnov CZ 30 C4
Titisee D 25 E2
Titovo Velenje SLO 37 F1
Tittling D 28 C3
Tittmoning D 28 B1
Titz D 12 C2
Tjæreborg DK 2 B4
Toblach/Dobbiaco I 36 A2
Todtmoos D 25 E1
Todtnau D 25 E1
Toftlund DK 2 C3
Tollarp S 5 D4
Tolmezzo I 36 C1
Tolmin SLO 37 D1
Tomelilla S 5 D3
Tommerup DK 3 D3
Tønder DK 2 B3
Tongeren (Tongres) B 12 B1
Tongres (Tongeren) B 12 B1
Tønning D 2 B1
Töpchin D 16 C3
Topoľčany SK 31 F2
Torgau D 16 C2
Torgelow D 11 D3
Torony H 38 C3
Torzym PL 17 F3
Tostedt D 8 C2
Toul F 24 B4
Toužim CZ 22 B2
Traben-Trarbach D 19 D3
Trafoi I 35 D2
Traisen A 30 B1
Traiskirchen A 30 C1
Traismauer A 30 B2
Trakošćan HR 38 B1
Tramelan CH 33 D4
Tranås S 5 D4
Tranderup DK 3 E2
Tranekaer DK 3 E3
Trassem D 18 C2
Traun A 29 E2
Traunkirchen A 37 D4
Traunreut D 28 B1
Traunstein D 28 B1
Travemünde D 9 E4
Travers CH 32 C3
Trebatsch D 17 D3
Trebbin D 16 C3
Třebenice CZ 23 D3
Třebíč CZ 30 B4
Třeboň CZ 29 F3
Treia D 2 C2
Treis D 19 D3
Trelleborg S 4 C3
Tremezzo I 34 A1
Třemošná CZ 22 C2
Trenčianska Turná SK 31 F3
Trenčín SK 31 F3
Trendelburg D 14 B2
Trento I 35 E1
Tresenda I 34 C1
Třešt CZ 30 A4
Treuchtlingen D 27 E3
Treuenbrietzen D 16 B3
Trhové Sviny CZ 29 E3
Triaucourt-en-Argonne F ... 24 A4
Triberg D 25 F2
Tribsees D 10 B4

Tricesimo I 36 C1
Trichiana I 36 A1
Trieben A 37 E3
Trier D 18 C2
Trittau D 9 D3
Trittenheim D 18 C2
Trnava SK 31 E2
Trocnov CZ 29 E3
Trofaiach A 37 F3
Trois-Ponts B 18 B4
Trojane SLO 37 F1
Tröstau D 21 F2
Trostberg D 28 B1
Trstin SK 31 E2
Truchtersheim F 25 E3
Trzcinno PL 11 F1
Trzcińsko Zdrój PL 11 E1
Trzebiatów PL 11 F4
Trzebiel PL 17 E2
Trzebież PL 11 E3
Tržič SLO 37 E1
Tschernitz D 17 E2
Tübingen D 26 B3
Tubre/Taufers I 35 D2
Tüchen D 10 A2
Tullebolle DK 3 E2
Tulln A 30 B2
Turckheim F 25 D2
Türkheim D 27 D2
Turnhout B 12 A2
Türnitz A 30 A1
Turnov CZ 23 F3
Turrach A 37 D2
Turzovka PL 31 F4
Tuttlingen D 26 A2
Tutzing D 27 E1
Tvrdošovce SK 31 F1
Twimberg A 37 F2
Twist D 7 E1
Twistringen D 8 B2
Týn nad Vltavou CZ 29 E4
Tzummarum NL 6 C3

U

Überlingen D 26 B1
Uchte D 8 B1
Uckange F 18 B1
Uden NL 12 B3
Ueckermünde D 11 D3
Uelsen D 7 D1
Uelzen D 9 D2
Uetersen D 8 C3
Uetze D 15 D4
Uffenheim D 20 C1
Ugerlose DK 4 A4
Ugine F 32 B1
Uherské Hradiště CZ 31 E3
Uherský Brod CZ 31 E3
Uhlířské Janovice CZ 23 E2
Uhřiněves CZ 23 E2
Uithoorn NL 6 A1
Uithuizen NL 7 D3
Ullersev DK 3 E3
Ulm D 26 C2
Ulmen D 19 D3
Ulstrup DK 3 F4
Umhausen A 35 D3
Úněšov CZ 22 C2
Unhošt' CZ 23 D2
Unna D 13 E2
Unter Pfaffenhofen D 27 E2
Unter-Schleissheim D 27 F2
Unterach A 36 C4
Unterlüss D 9 D1
Unteruhldingen D 26 B1
Unterwasser CH 34 B3
Unterweissenbach A 29 F2
Unterwössen D 36 B4
Urk NL 6 B2
Urnäsch CH 34 B3

57

Usedom D	11 D3
Usingen D	19 F3
Uslar D	14 C2
Usseln D	14 A2
Uštěk CZ	23 D3
Uster CH	34 A4
Ústí nad Labem CZ	23 D3
Uthlede D	8 B3
Utrecht NL	12 A4
Uttendorf A	36 B3
Uttendorf A	28 C2
Utting D	27 E1
Úvaly CZ	23 E2

V

Vaassen NL	6 C1
Vaduz FL	34 B3
Vaihingen D	26 B4
Valašská Polanka CZ	31 E4
Valašské Meziříčí CZ	31 E4
Valbella CH	34 B2
Valdahon F	32 B4
Valkenburg NL	12 B1
Valkenswaard NL	12 B2
Vallákra S	4 C4
Vallorbe CH	32 B3
Vallorcine F	32 C1
Vals CH	34 A2
Valtournenche I	33 D1
Vamdrup DK	2 C4
Vámosszabadi H	39 E4
Vandel DK	2 C4
Varallo I	33 E1
Varaždin HR	38 C1
Varde DK	2 B4
Varel D	8 A3
Varenna I	34 B1
Varnsdorf CZ	23 E4
Várpalota H	39 F3
Várpslöd H	39 E3
Varsseveld NL	12 C3
Vasvár H	39 D2
Vát H	39 D3
Vaucouleurs F	24 B3
Vauvillers F	24 B2
Veberöd S	5 D4
Vechta D	8 A1
Vedbaek DK	4 B4
Veendam NL	7 D3
Veenendaal NL	12 B4
Veghel NL	12 B3
Vejen DK	2 C4
Vejers Strand DK	2 B4
Vejle DK	3 D4
Vel'ké Leváre SK	31 D2
Vel'ke Ripňany SK	31 E2
Vel'ké Uherce SK	31 F2
Vel'ký Meder SK	39 E4
Velbert D	13 D2
Velburg D	27 F4
Velden A	37 D2
Velden D	21 E1
Velden D	28 B2
Veldhoven NL	12 B3
Velešín CZ	29 E3
Velká Bíteš CZ	30 C4
Velká Hled'sebe CZ	22 B2
Velká nad Veličkou CZ	31 E3
Velke Brezno CZ	23 D3
Velké Karlovice CZ	31 F4
Velké Meziříci CZ	30 B4
Velké Němčice CZ	30 C3
Velky Újezd CZ	31 E4
Vellinge S	4 C3
Velp NL	12 C4
Velpke D	15 E4
Veltrusy CZ	23 D2
Velvary CZ	23 D2
Vemmenaes DK	3 E3
Venlo NL	12 C2

Venray NL	12 C3
Venzone I	36 C1
Verbania-Pallanza I	33 F1
Verbier CH	32 C1
Verden D	8 B2
Verdun F	18 A1
Verl D	14 A3
Verny F	24 C4
Verrières-de-Joux F	32 B3
Versmold D	13 F3
Versoix CH	32 B2
Verviers B	18 B4
Vése H	39 D1
Veselí nad Lužnici CZ	29 F4
Veselí nad Moravou CZ	31 D3
Vesoul F	24 B1
Vester Egesborg DK	4 A3
Veszprém H	39 E2
Veszprémvarsány H	39 E3
Vetschau D	17 D2
Vevey CH	32 C2
Veyrier F	32 B1
Vézelise F	24 B3
Vezzano I	35 D1
Vianden L	18 B3
Vianen NL	12 A4
Vić SLO	37 F2
Viechtach D	28 C3
Vielsalm B	18 B3
Vienenburg D	15 D3
Viersen D	12 C2
Vierzehnheiligen D	21 E2
Vig DK	4 A4
Vigneulles F	18 A1
Vignory F	24 A3
Vik S	5 E4
Vilémov CZ	23 F2
Villa Santina I	36 B1
Villach A	37 D2
Villars CH	32 C2
Ville F	25 D3
Villers-le-Lac F	32 C3
Villersexel F	24 C1
Villingen D	25 F2
Vilsbiburg D	28 B2
Vilseck D	21 F1
Vilshofen D	28 C2
Vimperk CZ	29 D3
Vinzelberg D	15 F4
Vipiteno/Sterzing I	35 E2
Virgen A	36 B2
Virieu-le-Grand F	32 A1
Virton B	18 A2
Visbek D	8 A2
Visé B	12 B1
Viskinge DK	3 F4
Visp CH	33 E2
Visselhövede D	8 C2
Vissenbjerg DK	3 D3
Visz H	39 E2
Vitemolla S	5 E4
Vitis A	30 A3
Vittel F	24 B3
Vizovice CZ	31 E4
Vlachovo Březi CZ	29 D3
Vlagtweed NL	7 E2
Vlašim CZ	23 E1
Vlotho D	14 B4
Vöcklabruck A	29 D1
Vodňany CZ	29 E3
Vohburg D	27 F3
Vohenstrauss D	22 A1
Vöhringen D	26 C2
Void F	24 B4
Voitsberg A	38 A2
Vojens DK	2 C3
Vojnik SLO	38 A1
Vojtanov CZ	22 A2
Volary CZ	29 D3
Volders A	35 F3
Volendam NL	6 B2
Volkach D	20 C2
Völkermarkt A	37 E2
Völklingen D	18 C1

Volkmarsen D	14 B2
Volyně CZ	29 D4
Voorst NL	12 C4
Vorau A	38 B3
Vorbasse DK	2 C4
Vorchdorf A	29 D1
Vörden D	7 F1
Vordernberg A	37 F3
Vorderriss D	35 E4
Vordingborg DK	4 A2
Vorsfelde D	15 E4
Votice CZ	23 E1
Vráble SK	31 F2
Vransko SLO	37 F1
Vratno HR	38 C1
Vrbové SK	31 E2
Vrchlabí CZ	23 F3
Vreden D	13 D4
Vroomshoop NL	7 D1
Vroutek CZ	22 C2
Vsetin CZ	31 E4
Vught NL	12 B3
Výškov CZ	31 D4
Vyšší Brod CZ	29 E2

W

Waabs D	3 D2
Waalwijk NL	12 A3
Wabern D	14 B1
Wachow D	16 B4
Wächtersbach D	20 B3
Wackersdorf D	28 B4
Wädenswil CH	33 F3
Wagenfeld D	8 A1
Wageningen NL	12 B4
Waging D	28 B1
Wagrain A	36 C3
Wahlwies D	26 A1
Wahrenholz D	9 D1
Waiblingen D	26 B3
Waidhaus D	22 A1
Waidhofen an der Thaya D	30 A3
Waidhofen an der Ybbs A	29 F1
Waidring A	36 B4
Waischenfeld D	21 E2
Walbeck D	15 E4
Walchensee D	35 E4
Walchsee A	36 B4
Wald CH	34 A3
Waldbröl D	13 E1
Waldeck D	14 B2
Waldenbuch D	26 B3
Waldenburg D	22 B4
Waldfischbach D	19 D1
Waldheim D	16 C1
Waldkirch D	25 E2
Waldkirchen D	29 D3
Waldkraiburg D	28 B2
Waldmünchen D	28 B4
Waldowice PL	17 F4
Waldsassen D	22 A2
Waldshut D	25 E1
Walenstadt CH	34 B3
Walldorf D	19 F1
Walldürn D	20 B1
Wallenfels D	21 E3
Wallersdorf D	28 B3
Wallerstein D	27 D3
Wallsbüll D	2 C2
Walsrode D	8 C2
Waltrop D	13 E3
Wanderup D	2 C2
Wanfried D	14 C1
Wangen D	26 C1
Wangenbourg F	25 D3
Wangerooge D	7 F4
Wängi CH	34 A4
Wankendorf D	9 D4
Wanzleben D	15 F3

Warburg D	14 B2
Wardenburg D	8 A2
Waremme B	12 A1
Waren D	10 B3
Warendorf D	13 F3
Warin D	10 A3
Warmensteinach D	21 F2
Warnemünde D	10 B4
Warnsveld NL	12 C4
Warstein D	13 F2
Warth A	34 C3
Wartha D	15 D1
Wasselonne F	25 D3
Wassen CH	33 F2
Wassenberg D	12 C2
Wasseralfingen D	27 D3
Wasserbillig L	18 C2
Wasserburg D	28 A1
Wassertrüdingen D	27 D4
Wasungen D	21 D4
Wattens A	35 F3
Wattwil CH	34 B3
Waxweiler D	18 C3
Wedel D	8 C3
Weener D	7 E3
Weert NL	12 B2
Weesen CH	34 B3
Weeze D	12 C3
Wegberg D	12 C2
Wegeleben D	15 E3
Weggis CH	33 F3
Wegliniec PL	17 F1
Wegorzyno PL	11 F3
Wegscheid D	29 D2
Wehr D	19 D4
Wehr D	25 E1
Weichshofen D	28 B3
Weida D	22 A4
Weiden D	22 A1
Weidenberg D	21 F2
Weigetschlag A	29 E2
Weikersheim D	20 C1
Weil D	26 B3
Weilburg D	19 F4
Weilheim D	27 E1
Weimar D	21 E4
Weinfelden CH	34 B4
Weingarten D	26 C1
Weinheim D	19 F2
Weinsberg D	26 B4
Weismain D	21 E2
Weissbriach A	36 C2
Weissenbach A	35 D4
Weissenburg D	27 E3
Weissenfels D	16 A1
Weissenhorn D	26 C2
Weissenkirchen A	30 A2
Weissensee D	15 E1
Weissenstadt D	21 F2
Weisskirchen A	37 E3
Weisswasser D	17 E2
Weitendorf D	10 B3
Weitra A	29 F2
Weiz A	38 B3
Welden D	27 D2
Well NL	12 C3
Wellaune D	16 B2
Welle D	8 C2
Wellin B	18 A3
Wels A	29 D1
Welsberg/Monguelfo I	36 A2
Welschofen/ Nova Levante I	35 E1
Weltenburg D	28 A3
Welzheim D	26 C3
Wemding D	27 D3
Wemperhardt L	18 B3
Wengen CH	33 E2
Wenns A	35 D3
Weppersdorf A	38 C3
Werben D	10 A1
Werbomont B	18 B4
Werdau D	22 A4
Werder D	16 B4

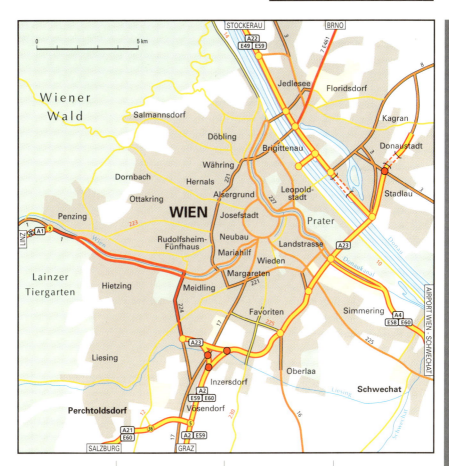

Werdohl D	13 E2	Weyer-Markt A	37 E4	Wilhelmshaven D	8 A3	Witnica PL	17 E4
Werfen A	36 C3	Weyhausen D	9 DI	Wilhering A	29 E2	Wittdün D	2 B2
Werl D	13 E2	Weyregg A	29 DI	Willingen D	14 A2	Witten D	13 E2
Werlte D	7 E2	Widuchowa PL	II E2	Willisau CH	33 E3	Wittenberge D	10 A2
Wermelskirchen D	13 D2	Wiedenbrück D	13 F3	Wilnsdorf D	13 FI	Wittenburg D	9 E3
Wernberg D	22 AI	Wiefelstede D	8 A3	Wilster D	8 C4	Wittichenau D	17 DI
Werne D	13 E3	Wiehe D	15 EI	Wiltz L	18 B3	Wittingen D	9 EI
Werneck D	20 C2	Wiek D	4 C2	Windeck D	13 EI	Wittlich D	18 C3
Werneuchen D	17 D4	Wien A	30 CI	Windisch D	22 A2	Wittmund D	7 F3
Wernigerode D	15 E3	Wiener Neustadt A	38 C4	Windischgarsten A	37 E4	Wittstock D	10 B2
Wertach D	35 D4	Wierden NL	7 DI	Windsbach D	27 E4	Witzenhausen D	14 C2
Wertheim D	20 B2	Wies D	35 E4	Winklern A	36 B2	Woerden NL	12 A4
Werther D	14 A3	Wiesau D	22 A2	Winnenden D	26 B3	Woerth F	25 E4
Wertingen D	27 D3	Wiesbaden D	19 F3	Winnigstedt D	15 D3	Wohlen CH	33 E4
Wesel D	13 D3	Wieselburg A	30 AI	Winnweiler D	19 E2	Woldegk D	II D2
Wesenberg D	10 C2	Wiesenburg D	16 B3	Winschoten NL	7 E3	Wolfach D	25 F2
Wesendorf D	9 DI	Wiesentheid D	20 C2	Winsen D	8 CI	Wolfegg D	26 CI
Wesselburen D	2 BI	Wiesloch D	19 FI	Winsen D	9 D3	Wolfen D	16 A2
Wessobrunn D	27 EI	Wiesmath A	38 C4	Winsum NL	7 D3	Wolfenbüttel D	15 D3
West-Terschelling NL	6 B3	Wiesmoor D	7 F3	Winterberg D	14 A2	Wolfhagen D	14 B2
Westendorf A	36 A3	Wietze D	8 CI	Winterfeld D	9 EI	Wolframs-Eschenbach D	27 E4
Westenholz D	8 CI	Wijhe NL	6 CI	Wintermoor D	8 C2	Wolfratshausen D	27 EI
Westensee D	3 DI	Wil CH	34 B4	Winterswijk NL	13 D4	Wolfsberg A	37 F2
Westerholt D	7 E3	Wildalpen A	37 F4	Winterthur CH	34 A4	Wolfsburg D	15 E4
Westerland D	2 B3	Wildbad D	26 A3	Wipperfürth D	13 E2	Wolfstein D	19 D2
Westerlo B	12 A2	Wildenrath D	12 C2	Wippra D	15 E2	Wolgast D	II D4
Westerstede D	7 F3	Wildeshausen D	8 A2	Wischhafen D	8 C4	Wolhusen CH	33 E3
Wetter D	13 E2	Wildhaus CH	34 B3	Wiselka PL	II E3	Wolin PL	II E3
Wettringen D	13 E4	Wildon A	38 A2	Wismar D	9 F4	Wolkenstein D	22 C3
Wetzikon CH	34 A4	Wilfersdorf A	30 C2	Wissembourg F	25 E4	Wolkenstein in Gardena/	
Wetzlar D	19 F4	Wilhelmsburg A	30 BI	Wissen D	13 EI	Selva di Val Gardena I	35 F2

59

Wolkersdorf A 30 C2
Wollersdorf A 38 C4
Wollin D 16 B3
Wolmirstedt D 15 F3
Wolnzach D 27 F3
Wolvega NL 6 C2
Worb CH 33 D3
Worbis D 15 D2
Wörgl A 36 A4
Workum NL 6 B2
Wörlitz D 16 B3
Wormerveer NL 6 A2
Worms D 19 F2
Wörrstadt D 19 E2
Wörth D 25 F4
Wörth D 20 B2
Wörth D 28 B3
Wredenhagen D 10 B2
Wriezen D 11 D1
Wulfen D 13 D3
Wullowitz A 29 E2
Wünnenberg D 14 A2
Wunsiedel D 21 F2
Wunstorf D 14 C4
Wuppertal D 13 D2
Wurzbach D 21 E3
Würzburg D 20 C2
Wurzen D 16 B1
Wust D 16 A4
Wusterhausen D 10 B1
Wüstermarke D 16 C2
Wustrow D 4 B1
Wyk D 2 B2

X

Xanten D 12 C3
Xertigny F 24 C2
Xhoffraix B 18 B4

Y

Ybbs an der Donau A 29 F1
Ybbsitz A 29 F1
Yenne F 32 A1
Yngsjö S 5 E4
Ystad S 5 D3
Yverdon-les-Bains CH 32 C3
Yvoire F 32 B2

Z

Zaandam NL 6 A1
Zaga SLO 36 C1
Zagań PL 17 F2
Zahna D 16 B3
Zákupy CZ 23 E3
Zalaapáti H 39 D2
Zalabaksa H 38 C2
Zalabér H 39 D2
Zalaegerszeg H 39 D2
Zalakomár H 39 D1
Zalalövö H 38 C2
Zalaszentbalázs H 39 D1
Zaltbommel NL 12 B3

Zamárdi H 39 E2
Zandvoort NL 6 A1
Zapfendorf D 21 D2
Zarrentin D 9 E3
Zary PL 17 F2
Zasieki PL 17 E2
Žatec CZ 22 C3
Zauchwitz D 16 C3
Zawada PL 17 F3
Zawidów PL 23 F4
Zbraslav CZ 23 D2
Zbraslavice CZ 23 F1
Ždar CZ 22 C2
Ždár nad Sázavou CZ 30 B4
Zdiby CZ 23 E2
Zdice CZ 23 D2
Zdounky CZ 31 D4
Zebrzydowa PL 17 F1
Zehdenick D 10 C1
Zeist NL 12 B4
Zeitz D 16 A1
Želetava CZ 30 B3
Železná Ruda CZ 28 C4
Železný Brod CZ 23 F3
Zeliv CZ 23 F1
Zell A 29 D2
Zell D 19 D3
Zell D 25 E1
Zell am See A 36 B3
Zell am Ziller A 35 F3
Zella-Mehlis D 21 D4
Želnava CZ 29 D3
Zeltweg A 37 E3
Zerbst D 16 A3

Zerf D 18 C2
Zermatt CH 33 D1
Zernez CH 34 C2
Zernien D 9 E2
Zetel D 7 F3
Zeulenroda D 21 F3
Zeven D 8 C3
Zevenaar NL 12 C4
Zgorzelec PL 17 F1
Zickhusen D 9 F3
Židlochovice CZ 30 C3
Ziegenrück D 21 F3
Zielona Góra PL 17 F3
Ziersdorf A 30 B2
Zierzow D 9 F2
Ziesar D 16 B3
Ziethen D 11 D3
Zinal CH 33 D1
Zingst D 4 B1
Zinnowitz D 11 D4
Zinnwald-Georgenfeld D 23 D3
Zirc H 39 E3
Zirchow D 11 D3
Zirl A 35 E3
Žirovnice CZ 30 A4
Zistersdorf A 31 D2
Zittau D 23 E4
Zizers CH 34 B3
Zlatá Koruna CZ 29 E3
Zlaté Moravce SK 31 F2
Žleby CZ 23 F2
Zliechov SK 31 F3
Zlín CZ 31 E4
Zlonice CZ 23 D3

Žlutice CZ 22 C2
Znojmo CZ 30 B3
Zoetermeer NL 12 A4
Zofingen CH 33 E4
Zolder B 12 A2
Zörbig D 16 A2
Zorge D 15 D2
Zorneding D 27 F1
Zossen D 16 C3
Zoutkamp NL 7 D3
Zschopau D 22 C4
Zudar D 10 C4
Zug CH 33 F3
Zuidhorn NL 7 D3
Zuidlaren NL 7 D2
Zülpich D 12 C1
Zundert NL 12 A3
Zuoz CH 34 C2
Zürich CH 33 F4
Zürs A 34 C3
Zurzach CH 25 F1
Zusmarshausen D 27 D2
Züsow D 10 A4
Zutphen NL 12 C4
Zweibrücken D 19 D1
Zweisimmen CH 33 D2
Zwettl A 30 A2
Zwettl an der Rodl A 29 E2
Zwickau D 22 B4
Zwiefalten D 26 B2
Zwiesel D 28 C3
Zwijndrecht NL 12 A4
Zwingenberg D 20 A1
Zwolle NL 6 C1